DRIVING FOR INSTRUCTORS
a practical training guide

DRIVING FOR INSTRUCTORS
a practical training guide

Graham Yuill, *ADI*

Otter Publications
Chichester, England

First published in 1996 by **Otter Publications**, 5 Mosse Gardens, Fishbourne, Chichester, West Sussex, PO19 3PQ.

The male pronoun has been used throughout this book. This is simply to avoid ugly or cumbersome language and no discrimination or bias is intended.

British Library Cataloging in Publication Data
A CIP record for this book is available from the British Library.
ISBN 1 899053 09 3

Acknowledgements
Grateful thanks to the Royal National Institute for the Deaf for their permission to reproduce the Standard Manual Alphabet, the DIA for the endorsement, and the DSA for permission to reproduce the Register of Approved Driving Instructors badge and the 10 ADI126PT/03 Preset Test Forms. The publisher would like to thank John E. Ayland, Chief Examiner DIAmond Advanced Motorists, formerly Deputy Chief Driving Examiner, Driving Standards Agency, Department of Transport, for his technical advice and proof reading skills.

Text design by Angela Hutchings.
Cover design by Jim Wilkie.
Printed and bound in Great Britain by Hartnolls Ltd., Bodmin.
Distributed in the UK by Grantham Book Services Ltd., Isaac Newton Way, Alma Park Industrial Estate, Grantham, Lincolnshire.
The Otter Publications logo is reproduced from original artwork by David Kitt.

Contents

Foreword

A driving instructor should be an ambassador for road safety.

Whilst the Driving Standards Agency are the regulators of our industry, the standards demanded have not been particularly high and therefore, all driving instructors should aim to improve their own driving and teaching skills way beyond the Grade 6 standard. In fact, nearly half of all ADIs are given the minimum grade to remain on the Register of Approved Driving Instructors.

The Driving Instructors Association is the industry's lead body for all driving instructors and can assist all those who are interested in becoming driving instructors, not only to gain their basic qualification, but to climb the ladder of success. Who knows, very soon you may be receiving the coveted Diploma in Driving Instruction (Dip. DI) or progress to a Bachelor of Science of BA in driver education. Yes, you can even achieve a Masters degree! The common denominator is having a will to driver properly and teach to a high standard.

Happy reading.

Graham R. J. Fryer
Chief Executive
Driving Instructors Association

Chapter 1

HOW TO BECOME A DEPARTMENT OF TRANSPORT APPROVED DRIVING INSTRUCTOR

This book will be an invaluable guide to you if you are studying for the Department of Transport's Approved Driving Instructor qualifying examination. It will assist you to give safe and skilful driving education to any learner driver from complete novice through to the driving test itself. Anyone who wants to become an Approved Driving Instructor (A.D.I.), must hold a full car driving licence for over 4 years, with no disqualifications. You must be a fit and proper person with no criminal convictions. Before you can give driving instruction for finance or reward you must be registered by the Department of Transport.

To qualify as a driving instructor you have to sit three very stringent exams. The first exam is a tough written examination which consists of 100 questions. For every question a choice of three answers is given. Only one of these three answers is correct, e.g. A driver must not sound the horn of his vehicle when it is moving in a built-up area between the hours of:

A. 23.00 and 06.30. **B.** 23.30 and 07.00. **C.** 22.30 and 06.00. Answer: **B**

The 100 questions will be split into 4 bands, consisting of 25 questions in each band. They are as follows:

Band 1 Road procedure. **Band 2** (a) Traffic signs and signals.
(b) Pedestrians. (c) Car control. (d) Mechanics.
Band 3 (a) Law. (b) Driving test. (c) Disabilities.
Band 4 (a) Instructional techniques. (b) Publications.

The syllabus of the written examination includes questions on the theory of learning and the theory and practice of teaching and assessment. A driving instructor is a teacher and he/she should know the basic principles of this skill. You must achieve a minimum mark in each band of 80% and an overall mark of 85% to pass.

If you are successful at the written examination you will be invited to sit an advanced driving test. This will be conducted by a supervising examiner from the Driving Standards Agency and a high standard of driving is expected. If you pass the driving test you will be eligible to sit the final examination. This will test your ability to give practical driving instruction to a supervising examiner acting as a learner driver. You must pass the written examination before applying for the test of driving technique, and you must pass this before applying for the test of instructional ability.

If you sit the test of instructional ability which is divided into two phases, the supervising examiner will indicate to you the level of learner experience he is imitating. This will be either a novice (phase 1 pupil) or a learner who is near driving test standard (phase 2 pupil). To qualify you must pass all three parts within 2 years. However, if you fail to do so you will have to restart from the beginning. After passing the initial written examination, you will be allowed to make only 3 attempts at each of the subsequent driving and instructional ability tests within the 2 year period. If you fail, you will have to wait until the 2 year period ends before starting to qualify again. This is to prevent candidates passing through familiarity instead of clear ability.

THE PRINCIPLES OF INSTRUCTION AND METHODS OF APPLICATION

Learning and remembering are voluntary processes and the instructor must endeavour to gain the learner's full co-operation from the start. Learner drivers will co-operate and try hard if:

- They are interested.
- There is an incentive.
- They can see the reason for doing an exercise or learning a skill.

Driving education is a science and driving is an art. It is essential that a driving instructor has a thorough knowledge of his subject to be successful. He must also be aware of the following guidelines which must apply according to circumstances.

The principles of good driving instruction are as follows:

- Aim.
- Planning and preparation.
- Interest and enthusiasm.
- Simplicity.
- Progress checks.

Aim

All driving education must be purposeful. The immediate aims are progress targets set for each individual lesson. The ultimate aim is to teach a learner how to drive safely and competently on the roads without any supervision.

The instructor must ask himself before giving a lesson, *"What is my aim and how is it to be obtained?"* To achieve this, you should divide each aim into individual objectives, which the learner should strive for during each lesson. Exercise techniques must be thoroughly known, such as the facts and the skills.

Planning and preparation

Each driving lesson must be well planned and careful preparation is most important. Time spent taken on preparation will be well rewarded, providing the instructor does not "over-do" the preparation by not being adaptable. Poor preparation will undoubtedly lead to a muddled and inefficiently conducted lesson.

The amount of preparation required will largely depend on the knowledge and experience of the instructor. You must assess each learner accordingly and plan your lesson to meet his individual needs.

Interest and enthusiasm

The driving instructor must be an enthusiast in his subject. He must also be interested in all aspects of his work and must constantly strive to improve his own knowledge and ability. Convince the learner that you have a genuine interest in their progress. However, the instructor should keep his enthusiasm under control and avoid becoming fanatical.

The driving instructor must keep his pupils interested if he is to obtain results. It is important that the instructor exploits the natural curiosity of his pupils and encourages them to think things out for themselves. After the learner has been told to carry out a manoeuvre, the instructor must get them to explain **why** they had to carry out the exercise. This is to ensure that the learner is not learning things "parrot-fashion". They must fully understand the necessity of the commands and if they do this it will help to mould them into safer drivers for the future. The learner may say that he fully understands what you have taught him. However, be careful as he may lie to avoid appearing foolish, or he may be trying to please you.

Simplicity

The driving instructor should make his instructions and explanations simple. Questions should be short and straight to the point. The key points should stand out clearly and he should worry about the variables later on, once the learner has grasped the important points. Technical words and phrases may be used but they must be clearly explained to the learner. However, at the same time the instructor must realise that the standard of intelligence and knowledge will vary from pupil to pupil, and so he must adapt his instructions accordingly. In other words, study the mental outlook of learners.

Progress checks

In driving instruction as well as in all other instructional subjects, the learner's progress must be checked at various stages to ensure that the learner is absorbing knowledge and acquiring skills. Weak points

must be noted and eliminated wherever possible. Stron͵
also be noted and use made of them. It is of vital in
progression stages are planned for each individual lear.
ability to instruct varies, proficiency is only obtained by
technique and by practicing its application.

BODY LANGUAGE/MANNER

Body language includes:- movements, posture, sitting position, use of
the arms, facial expression, eye movements, distance from others
(territories), dress etc. It is important to be able to interpret a learner
driver's body language and to be able to master your own body
language and realise its relevance to the message you wish to put
across. A driving instructor must have a pleasing manner. This means
the instructor's way of speaking, moving and gesturing when
conducting a lesson. His job is to speak clearly, distinctly and
emphatically. An instructor must be an understanding person and he
must be aware of and understand the many problems a learner driver
will come across whilst learning the difficult art of driving. An
instructor should avoid:

- Sarcasm.
- Bullying.
- Slang.
- Nagging.
- Mannerisms and nervous gestures.

*A driving instructor must know his stuff, never bluff and always
practice what he preaches!*

STARTING AND ENDING WITH AN OBJECTIVE

When giving instruction to a learner driver you must structure your
method of teaching and explain everything in a systematic and logical
way. Your objective is to try to get the learner to be successful in
everything he does. In other words the learning conditions must be

within the learner's ability to handle difficult situations (for example, you wouldn't use Piccadilly Circus as a learner's first roundabout). It is important that every lesson should set an objective. This should be stated by the instructor in the introduction to the lesson. The aim of any method of teaching must be to ensure that learning takes place. The instruction given must be clear and easy to understand. All faults must be **identified, analysed** and **corrected**. The lesson should end with an objective achieved and the instructor should set an objective for the next lesson especially if it is to be structured on what has been learnt.

It is important to remember an objective may change according to circumstances. For example, assume you told the learner that the objective of the lesson was to drive to a particular area to practice reversing around a corner. Whilst driving to the location the learner commits a serious fault when making a right turn by cutting in front of a car, causing it to swerve. Since the learner has made a serious fault, and another road user has been involved, you must change your objective immediately and concentrate on a new objective. You should draw the learner's attention to the serious fault and make the necessary corrections before practicing the reverse exercise.

QUESTION AND ANSWER TECHNIQUE

You must question the learner prior to conducting a lesson on any subject. The type of questions you should ask will depend on the standard of the learner. Therefore, it is very important that you find out what the learner knows and can do. Question the learner in order to get "feed back". This allows you to fully gauge his level of understanding and is commonly known as the "Question and Answer" technique. Avoid asking 'Yes/No' questions which have a 50/50 chance of being correct. For example do not ask, *"Would you normally position your car about 90 cm away when passing parked vehicles?"* (a closed question). It would be better to say, *"What position would you normally adopt when passing parked vehicles?"* (an open question). Begin questions with, *why, how, what, if, where, when or which*. To promote pupil participation, the learner should be encouraged to ask **you** questions which are relevant to the lesson you are teaching. Learners suffer from the following types of fault:

Teaching fault

The learner does not know how to carry out the exercise because they have never been shown how to perform it properly.

Practice fault

The learner has been taught the exercise properly but he does not fully understand the rudiments of the exercise. This may not happen frequently, but the learner may slip in and out of practice faults. You must ensure that they have perfected the routine at all times. You may have to break things down into component parts, to ensure that all sections of the exercise are carried out correctly.

Attitude fault

If the learner suffers from this type of fault, you should solve the problem at once. For example, assume the learner persistently drives at a speed in excess of the speed limit. You should use tact, and convince the learner that his persistent excessive speed is often caused by lack of awareness of actual or potential danger or poor perception of speed because he is a regular passenger in a fast-driven car. You should therefore look for and treat the **cause** of the error rather than the effect. However, if the fault is less obvious to pinpoint, "diagnostic questioning" can be used with great success.

TYPES OF BRIEFING

There are two types of briefing which can be given to a learner driver; instructional and directional.

The instructional briefing (phase 1)

This briefing is given when the topic of the lesson you are teaching contains material which is new to the learner. It should contain all of the key or important learning points which must be fully explained, and they are listed throughout the book.

The directional briefing (phase 2)
This briefing is less complex and it is normally given if the subject of the lesson has been taught to the learner before. Before undertaking any exercise it is important that you fully explain to the learner exactly what is expected of him. You should not waste time teaching something which has already been taught unless the learner still has problems in this area. Once you know the learner's level of competence (phase 1 or phase 2) and you have decided which type of briefing you are going to give, you should brief the learner fully, demonstrating where required, before allowing him to practice himself. Ideally, you should be aiming for the learner to do the manoeuvre correctly from the outset. If you are teaching a learner who is a phase one pupil it will be easier for him to achieve this if you talk him through each stage of the exercise. Eventually, the learner will be able to perform the manoeuvre without being talked through.

TRANSFERRED RESPONSIBILITY
You should be able to gauge at what stage during the learning process the learner is ready to make decisions and take over the responsibility for his actions from yourself.

KEEPING THINGS SIMPLE
Do not "waffle" when giving an explanation. Try to keep everything as short and as simple as possible, and avoid becoming too technical. If you are too technical or give long boring explanations the learner will lose interest and his concentration will wander. Never expect a learner to perform at a high standard if he has only received a few driving lessons. Rome was not built in a day. If your pupil is a slow learner, reassure him that mistakes are quite natural and with more practice he will succeed eventually. Older students usually take longer

to learn to drive, preferring to learn at their own pace. They also tend to be more anxious and their reaction times are usually slower.

ROUTE PLANNING

Before commencing any lesson you must decide which type of route would best suit the learner. Careful preparation of each route is most important. Routes are classified into 3 groups:

- Nursery.
- Intermediate.
- Advanced.

The type of route you choose will mainly depend on the ability of the learner and you should take into account the driving skills or procedures to be taught. You wouldn't allow a complete beginner to practice changing gear along Oxford Street. In the very early stages stick to nursery routes which should consist of fairly straight roads with very few parked vehicles (the latter may alarm the learner). When the learner has gained more confidence, you should switch to intermediate routes containing various types of road junctions, traffic lights, roundabouts and hills. Finally, when the learner has reached a high standard of driving, proceed to advanced routes. This should include one way streets, various types of dual carriageways, pedestrian/level crossings, etc.

INSTRUCTIONAL JARGON

Try to keep the instructions as brief and as simple as possible. If you follow the correct phraseology from the outset, the learner will eventually become accustomed to your style and will be able to follow the driving examiner's verbal instructions when sitting the driving test. If however, the car is in motion and your instructions are too long-winded, the learner will not have sufficient time to react. Remember, your car will cover a distance of 14 metres in one second if you are travelling at a speed of 30 mph. Therefore, try to give your instructions at least 92 metres (100 yards) before any junction.

To enable the learner to carry out all your instructions in good time, you will have to give your commands clearly and without rushing. If you fail to do this, the learner may panic, the car may approach the hazard too fast, and you may be forced to activate the dual controls in order to avoid an accident.

The importance of consistent terminology (particularly in the early stages of tuition) cannot be over emphasised. If your terminology is not consistent the learner will eventually become confused and may interpret you incorrectly, with potentially dangerous consequences. When the car is in motion, always keep an eye on what he is doing and be aware of the general road and traffic conditions, making full use of peripheral vision. You should adopt the following procedures:

- Assess the road.
- Eyes on pupil.
- Give instruction.
- Check mirror, signal.
- Check pupil's feet.
- Eyes on the road to check your position.

ROUTE DIRECTIONS
As soon as the learner is driving you will have to give directions. You should always direct the learner in a clear and unmistakable manner. Avoid telling a learner to turn right and left at "traffic lights", or to turn at "road junctions" (an in-built instructor fault) because when a learner is sitting his driving test the driving examiner will not point out the obvious. It is the learner's responsibility to be aware of the traffic lights or road junctions and to act accordingly. Avoid using the words 'go on' or 'carry on' - these terms may be interpreted literally and the learner may ignore traffic lights, road markings or give way rules.

TYPES OF ERRORS AND METHODS OF CORRECTION

You will find that learners make many mistakes whilst driving, so it is vital to spot and correct them. Learner mistakes fall into three categories.

The Minor Fault

A minor fault does not involve dangerous or potentially dangerous situations. This fault would not result in failure in the Driving Test. Minor faults can be corrected whilst the learner is driving e.g. *"You did not check your mirror before signalling"*. Even during the initial period of learning you should not permit the learner to commit minor faults. A minor fault will eventually lead to a serious or dangerous fault. If minor faults are not corrected from the outset and drawn to the learner's attention, he will be confused during the latter stages of the learning process. Should the learner keep making the same minor faults during his tuition, it is obvious that the dangers and consequences have not been clarified and you should solve the problem before rigor mortis sets in!

The Serious Fault

A serious fault involves potential danger, i.e. situations in which the learner's actions involve an unacceptable risk either to himself or others. If the learner makes a serious fault you must tell him to pull up at a convenient place on the left-hand side of the road (never allow the learner to stop in an unsafe place). Tell him what he did wrong and what he should have done, relaying your message in a clear and concise manner. Stick to the key learning points and worry about the less important items later, once the main points have been grasped. Don't try to give detailed explanations or corrections whilst the learner is driving as they can't take in detailed information whilst concentrating on the road. Should the learner be unsuccessful during the test, the examiner will transfer all the serious faults onto a Driving Test Report Form (DL25).

Dangerous Fault

A dangerous fault involves actual danger - you may even have to use the dual brake, or grab the steering wheel to avoid an accident. Always remember, if you ever have to activate the dual controls you must inform the learner why you had to do so, and what the consequences could have been if they had not been used. If a learner commits just one **DANGEROUS** fault during the driving test, the examiner will fail him automatically. If a learner commits any faults during his driving test, the driving examiner will evaluate the seriousness of the fault and the consequences of the fault especially on all other road users.

BE TACTFUL

Try to be tactful and avoid excessive or destructive criticism. For example, assume the learner commits a serious fault by turning a corner too widely.

Don't say, *"That was a stupid and serious mistake you committed back at that last junction - you turned too widely, and you could have collided with another vehicle. Don't do that again!"* It would be far better to say, *"At the last junction you turned too widely which could have been dangerous. How can we do it better?"*

CAUSES OF ERRORS

The majority of mistakes which occur during the initial period of learning are due to sheer inexperience and lack of knowledge. The most common causes of error are as follows:

- Insufficient knowledge.
- Contradictory knowledge (e.g. "My father said").
- Inadequate perception (not being aware of sensory information).
- Inadequate manual control.
- Poor health - tiredness, stress etc.

All faults committed by the learner during the driving test are recorded on a marking sheet by the driving examiner. The standards are laid down by the Driving Standards Agency and the examiner must follow them accordingly.

DUAL CONTROLS
The dual controls are primarily used to prevent the following:

- The risk of injury or damage to persons or property.
- An action which would be illegal.
- Excessive stress to the learner if unexpected situations arise.
- Mechanical damage to the car.

Usually a verbal instruction will be sufficient if given early enough. However, if the command is not obeyed you may need to take direct action. You should also try to anticipate the learner's intentions and be prepared to take evasive action if you feel at any time he is not under complete control. You must act before it is too late - remember, *it's better to be safe than sorry*.

Using the dual footbrake
- Always keep your right foot freely available for the footbrake, with the least amount of movement.
- If you see danger, locate the dual footbrake.
- Before using your footbrake, always check your dual mirror.
- Avoid fidgeting with the dual footbrake as this may alarm the pupil.
- After using the dual controls, explain to the pupil why you found it essential to use them.
- You can sometimes use the dual footbrake in order to reduce speed. This allows the learner more time to turn the steering wheel if he gets into an awkward situation.

POINTS TO REMEMBER

- When teaching you should avoid excessive verbal instruction or instruction lacking clarity, as this usually means that the instructor is not sure of his subject.
- You must be tactful and have a delicate perception of the feelings of others. You must show confidence, and give encouragement or praise when deserved.
- You may have to repeat things over and over again until it is understood fully. Be patient and understanding as you will succeed eventually.
- Excessive or destructive criticism will inhibit the learner's progress and destroy his confidence. Always remember, *"The Art is difficult, but criticism is easy"* (see figure 1).

Figure 1. Avoid excessive or destructive criticism.

If the learner asks you any questions you must answer them correctly and as simply as possible. In other words if a learner asks you the time don't tell him how the clock works. You should show pictures or draw diagrams to help get your answers across. Remember, *"A picture paints a thousand words"* (see figure 2).

- When teaching, you must avoid "Information Overload". In other words the learner becomes overwhelmed with so much information that he ends up learning nothing at all. Excessive detail will cause the learner's concentration to wander.
- The learner will learn much more quickly by doing things himself.
- If the learner gets bored, ask questions to keep him interested.
- If a driving instructor expects a low standard, this will slow the learner's progress.

The ultimate goal is for the learner to take over full responsibility and decision making from yourself and perform any exercise to the required standard. However, should problems still remain, you should consider varying your methods of instruction to suit the learner's individual needs.

Figure 2. If a learner asks you the time, don't tell him how the clock works!

USE YOUR IMAGINATION
You should not be frightened to use imaginative metaphors in order to capture the learner's attention and to etch important principles in his memory. For example, if edging out of a blind give way junction, encourage him to use "giraffe-like extensions" of his neck in order to see approaching traffic as early as possible (see figure 3).

HIGHWAY CODE AND OTHER MOTORING MATTERS

Many learners dislike learning the Highway Code. This must be discouraged as some learners will not fully comprehend road situations. Encourage the learner to study the Highway Code and other motoring matters from the outset and possibly test the learner with questions, to prepare him for the theory driving test (see Behind the Wheel - the learner driver's handbook). Always follow the three F's:

- Be Fair.
- Be Firm.
- Be Friendly.

Figure 3. Tell the learner to make giraffe-like extensions of the neck when emerging from a blind give way junction.

The most effective way to teach a learner driver with limited experience is to follow a basic pattern. The rules for effective teaching can be remembered by the following code:

- Explain.
- Demonstrate.   **(Phase 1)**
- Practice.
- Validate.

Explain

Inform the learner exactly what you want him to achieve before he starts any new exercise (show pictures or draw diagrams). If you do not, the learner will be unsure of what is expected and he will be unable to monitor his own progress adequately. Remember, stick to the key learning points and worry about the variables once the learner has grasped the important points. Avoid information overload.

Demonstrate

Always ask the learner if he would like a practical demonstration - this will reinforce what you have previously taught. Some learners tend to learn much more quickly if they actually see a demonstration.

Remember the adage, *"What I hear I forget, what I see I remember, what I do, I know".* Bear in mind that you do not always have to give a physical demonstration. However you could assist with any of the major controls if necessary, e.g. footbrake, clutch, steering (partial demonstration). In certain cases, when a wrong method must be shown or when a learner has to be shown why a certain movement must not be performed, a demonstration of the correct method should immediately follow. This will leave the correct impression in the learner's mind.

Practice

Talk the learner through the exercise and let him practice what he has just learned as this will establish his performance level. Ideally, the learner should improve with each lesson and eventually carry out the exercise with less and less instruction.

Validate

Recap at the end of the lesson, by means of a question and answer technique to see how much the learner has assimilated. Give feedback and plenty of encouragement, pointing out where progress has been made and where more practice is needed. Be very patient as you may have to go over points time and time again until the learner fully understands the subject. The ultimate goal is for the learner to take over full responsibility and decision making from yourself and perform the exercise to the required standard. However, should problems still remain you may have to consider varying your methods of instruction to suit the learner.

INSPIRE CONFIDENCE
There is always something to praise in every lesson with even the slowest of learners. Don't think of trial and error, think of trial and success. Be positive - not negative. When a learner does something right - tell him. Giving praise and encouragement will always help to boost the learner's confidence. Avoid excessive or destructive criticism.

THE TEST STANDARD PUPIL
Although the learner may have reached test standard (phase 2), it does not necessarily mean that his instruction is over or that he fully understands the subject. Areas of difficulty will probably remain and it is the instructor's responsibility to guide and give advice to the learner in the most effective way possible. The best procedure to use for a learner driver who has achieved a high standard can be remembered by the following code:

- Question.
- Observe.   **(Phase 2)**
- Explain.
- Practice/validate.

Question
Try to establish if the learner has any areas of difficulty. Ask him if he has any problems with the subject. Find out exactly what the learner knows, and what he is capable of. Ask two or three questions relevant to the procedure involved. For example, when dealing with crossroads you could ask, *"Do you understand the rules governing*

'nearside' and 'offside' and checking into your new road for danger?"

Observe
Set an objective, let the pupil drive and watch the learner to see if there are any mistakes and prompt only if absolutely necessary.

Explain
If there are any areas of difficulty, you should get to the root of the problem by giving a partial briefing, demonstrating where necessary.

Practice/validate
Let the learner practice with some instruction to eliminate any faults. Recap at the end of the lesson to evaluate the pupil's progress, discussing good and bad points. Give the learner feedback of their progress and encouragement.

LEARNING PLATEAU
A learner may reach a level of attainment where he/she appears not to be progressing any further. This is commonly known as the learning plateau. This presents a dilemma for the instructor, especially if the learner's attainment falls short of test standard. The learner may simply be demotivated and lack self-interest in developing any further.

When this situation arises the instructor should adopt an approach to encourage the learner to develop and extend current knowledge and skills sufficient for achieving test standard. A simple, yet effective example would be to place a monetary sum, such as £20 on the vehicle dashboard. The instructor would explain to the learner that for each serious or minor fault noted throughout the duration of the lesson, a £1 deduction would be made from the sum. The remainder at the end of the lesson will be given to the pupil.

This example allows the instructor to develop the pupil's current skills whilst also providing an effective motivating tool to an otherwise unenthusiastic pupil.

PART 3 TEST OF INSTRUCTIONAL ABILITY

The examiner will select 1 subject out of each of the 2 lists of the following topics (PST denotes pre-set test). See *pages 129 -139* for the marking sheets/failure forms used for the ten pre-set tests.

Subjects designated in phase 1 - Safety precautions on entering the car and explanation of the controls (**PST No. 1**), Moving off and stopping (**PST No. 2**), Turn in-the-road (**PST No. 3**), Reversing to the right or left (**PST No. 4**), Emergency stop and mirrors (**PST No. 5**), Dealing with pedestrian crossings and giving signals by indicators/arm as appropriate (**PST No. 6**), Approaching junctions to turn either right or left (**PST No. 7**), Dealing with emerging at road junctions (**PST No. 8**), Dealing with crossroads (**PST No. 9**), Meet, overtake and cross other traffic, allowing adequate clearance for other road users and anticipation (**PST No. 10**).

Subjects designated in phase 2 - Dealing with crossroads (**PST No. 1**), Meet, overtake and cross other traffic, allowing adequate clearance for other road users and anticipation (**PST Nos. 2 & 8**), Approaching junctions to turn either right or left (**PST No. 3**), Dealing with emerging at road junctions (**PST No. 4**), Making progress and general road positioning (**PST Nos 5 & 10**), Reverse parking (**PST No. 6**), Dealing with pedestrian crossings and giving signals by indicators/arm as appropriate (**PST Nos. 7 & 9**).

The minimum level for a pass is a grade 4 (grade 6 is the highest) in each phase. You must achieve a satisfactory grade in each phase on the same occasion to obtain an overall pass in the examination.

The part 3 test is comprised of 2 phases, each phase lasting about 30 minutes. It is vital to concentrate on the most important aspects of the subject chosen by the examiner. Phase 1 involves giving driving instruction to the examiner, acting either as a complete novice or a partly trained pupil. Phase 2 involves assessing and correcting the examiner, impersonating a pupil at about driving test standard.

Chapter 2

Lesson 1 - The safety checks and controls of the car

When the learner enters the car for the first time, you should start by teaching him certain safety checks followed by the major, minor, and auxiliary controls of the car. It is important that he knows where all the controls are within his car. You should talk him through these controls step-by-step. To avoid this lesson becoming a boring one-sided lecture, keep the learner interested by asking him some simple questions. The learner must carry out the following safety checks when he enters the car. They can easily be remembered by the following code:

- **DOORS**
- **SEAT**
- **STEERING WHEEL**   **(D.S.S.S.M.)** (see figure 4).
- **SEATBELT**
- **MIRRORS**

During the first lesson the learner may be excited and anxious to get started. Therefore, you should concentrate mainly on the foot and hand controls as initially these are more important for the learner to understand. The controls lesson should last approximately 40 minutes for a complete beginner. If however the learner has had previous driving experience, you should cut the controls lesson to approximately 15 minutes (sufficient to let him assimilate enough information prior to moving off). It is important that the teaching is properly timed to enable the learner to move off and stop the car during this first lesson. You must be prepared to answer any questions asked by the learner. Try to answer the questions as simply as possible and avoid becoming too technical - do not "waffle".

Once the learner is seated, tell him to check that the vehicle is secure by ensuring that the parking brake is applied. You must make sure that the learner knows how to open and close the doors properly and that he physically checks them. Ensure that the learner also checks and adjusts his seat, seatbelt and mirrors (see figure 4). Explain to the learner that the exterior mirrors help to reduce blind spots. They are used in conjunction with the interior mirror, and they must always be used before overtaking or passing stationary vehicles.

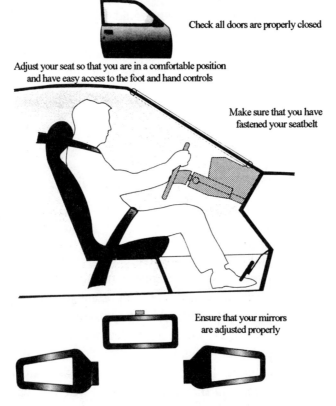

Check all doors are properly closed

Adjust your seat so that you are in a comfortable position and have easy access to the foot and hand controls

Make sure that you have fastened your seatbelt

Ensure that your mirrors are adjusted properly

Figure 4. The safety checks to be carried out before starting the engine.

After you have explained the safety checks, you should explain the main controls. The main controls are dealt with under two sections: the controls which are operated with the feet, and the controls operated with the hands. The foot controls are the accelerator, brake and clutch. Think of ABC. The hand controls are the gear lever, parking brake and steering wheel. Permit the learner to practice stationary gear changing, using the clutch down/off gas method as previously mentioned. Avoid doing it too often as this could flood the engine of your car and it will be difficult to re-start it. Point this out to the learner (see figure 5).

Figure 5. Changing gear.

It is a good idea to have an old steering wheel or circular disc handy in the car to demonstrate the "push and pull" method for steering because learners tend to cross their hands whilst steering. If this happens they may lose control and an accident may occur. If the learner wishes to turn left the most simple and effective way to teach this is to think of the face of a clock. The left hand should be moved to about eleven o'clock position and the wheel should be pulled downwards, whilst the right hand is slid down the wheel on the opposite side. The learner should then push up with the right hand whilst the left hand slides up the wheel. The movements are reversed for a right turn.

Moreover, although it may seem ridiculous, you should also inform the learner that the car must be straightened up after the car has turned the corner. The steering wheel must be fed back through the hands in the opposite direction, using the same "push and pull" method. Never allow the steering wheel to spin back on its own because the driver will not have full control of the car (see figure 6).

You should allow the learner to move his foot from the gas to the brake pedal a few times, without looking down at his feet, keeping the heel on the floor if possible. This will allow him to judge the distance his foot must travel between the two pedals (see figures 7 and 8). Ensure that the learner checks the gear lever is in neutral before starting the engine.

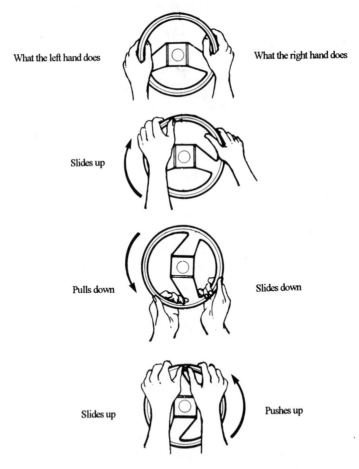

What the left hand does

What the right hand does

Slides up

Pulls down

Slides down

Slides up

Pushes up

Figure 6. The "push and pull method".

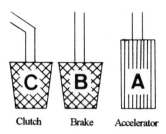

Figure 7. The foot controls.

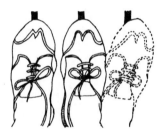

**Figure 8. Practice moving your feet from the footbrake to the accelerator
without looking down.**

Encourage the learner to practice using the accelerator (with the
engine running), until he is able to achieve a constant lively hum. If
there is a Rev. Counter, the learner should aim to set the engine speed
at 1500 - 2000 rpm. You should use the following terminology when
referring to the accelerator pedal:

- Set gas - gently apply pressure to the accelerator pedal.
- More gas - gently push the accelerator pedal down more.
- Less gas - gently ease your foot off the accelerator pedal.
- Off gas - remove your foot completely off the accelerator pedal.

It is crucial that the learner understands that free play at the top of the brake pedal does not activate the brakes. You should use the following terminology when referring to the brake pedal:

- Cover brake - place your foot over the pedal but don't touch.
- Gently brake - apply firm pressure to the footbrake.
- Gently brake to a stop - apply firm pressure to the footbrake until all four wheels come to a complete stop.

Explain in **simple** detail the mechanics which take place whilst the clutch is used when driving. Show or draw a simple diagram in order to get your message across. You may have to demonstrate "biting point", emphasising "feel" of clutch beginning to bite. Get the learner to practice this until he understands the principles of the exercise.

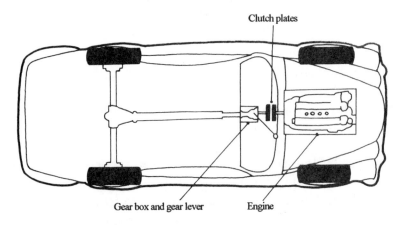

Figure 9. The workings of the clutch.

Use the following terminology when referring to the clutch pedal:

- Cover clutch - place your foot over the pedal but don't touch.
- Clutch down - push the clutch right down to the floor.
- Slowly clutch up - until the engine note changes then keep both feet still.

After explaining the foot controls, explain the 3 main types of hand controls:

- Gear lever and gears.
- Parking brake.
- Steering wheel.

Tell the learner that the approximate speeds for changing up are:

- 1st gear - between 0-10 mph approximately (a power gear).
- 2nd gear - between 10-20 mph approx. (a working gear).
- 3rd gear - between 20-30 mph approx. (a working gear).
- 4th gear - above 30 mph (a cruising gear).

The approximate speeds for changing down are:

- From 4th - 3rd gear - 20 mph.
- From 3rd - 2nd gear - 10 mph.
- From 2nd - 1st gear - under 5 mph.

Fifth gear
Inform the learner that the fifth gear should normally be selected when the car is travelling at approximately 50 mph. It is an economy gear to save fuel. In other words it give the car longer legs. Since the car is already moving at a fast speed the momentum of the car itself is enough to push it forward with very little help from the engine.

Making proper use of gears
Inform the learner that gears are used to make the car go faster and they assist the car to slow down in conjunction with the footbrake. By changing up the gears at the correct time he will save petrol and avoid wear and tear on the engine. The learner should listen to the sound of the engine to determine when to make a gear change. The gears which should be used are dependent on the learner's speed. The

slower the speed, the lower the gear: the higher the speed, the higher
the gear. The learner should be taught to change gear without looking
down at the gear lever.

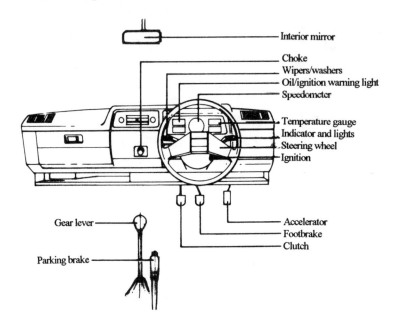

Figure 10. The minor and auxiliary controls.

The parking brake (*often referred to as the hand brake*)

Explain to the learner that the parking brake is used to secure the car
when it is stationary, by locking the two rear wheels. The parking
brake is normally found on the left-hand side of the driver's seat and
is operated by the left hand. The parking brake is also used for safety
reasons - for instance, when the car has been parked on a gradient,
when it has stopped at traffic lights, pedestrian crossings, or queuing
behind other vehicles, unless you are likely to be waiting for a very
short period of time. If the learner is bumped from behind the parking
brake will stop the car from being pushed forward. You should use
the following terminology when referring to the parking brake:

- Prepare the parking brake - hand on the parking brake ready to release it.
- Release the parking brake - hand on the parking brake lift it slightly pressing in the button, then simply push it down and release the button.
- Apply the parking brake - hand on the parking brake pressing in the button, then pull it up and release the button.

Encourage the learner to keep the button pressed in when he applies the parking brake. If he fails to do this he may cause damage to the ratchet. The learner should never apply the parking brake when the car is moving as this will lock the rear wheels and the car may skid. The parking brake can also be used in an emergency if the footbrake fails.

Steering wheel
Explain to the learner that the steering wheel normally works directly on the front wheels and changes the direction of the car to the right or the left. He should hold the steering wheel with both hands, lightly but firmly and to avoid wrapping his thumbs around the rim. Imagine the steering wheel as a clock and he should place his hands in a position corresponding to the hands on a clock face, either quarter to three or a ten to two, whichever is most comfortable (see figure 11). Instruction given to a beginner (phase 1) should include the following:

- Enter and leave the car safely (safety of opening doors).
- Carry out cockpit drill e.g. doors, parking brake, seat, mirrors, seatbelt; assume a correct seating posture and grip of the steering wheel.
- Start the engine, taking suitable precautions beforehand.
- Locate and identify the function of the main driving controls - *accelerator - footbrake - clutch - parking brake - gears - steering - indicators*.

Hands at the ten to two position   Hands at the quarter to three position

Figure 11. Holding the steering wheel.

Explain the MSM routine and give simple instructions for moving off, changing gear, steering and stopping in a safe, legal and convenient place. It is important that you keep your explanations simple and precise. The learner will only be able to absorb a certain amount of information. An inexperienced instructor will attempt to teach too much and judge his own performance by this. It is not important how much a learner has been taught, it is what he has learnt that counts. Tell the learner one thing at a time and do not proceed any further until you are satisfied that he can carry out all your instructions satisfactorily.

Ensure that the learner is fully aware of all the car's minor controls, in case he has to make use of them in the driving test. It is the responsibility of every driver to familiarise himself with the controls and instruments of a vehicle before driving it. The learner should also practice operating the indicator switch from a stationary position without taking his hands off the steering wheel.

Lesson 2 - Moving off, gear changing and stopping

In the early stages of driving the learner may find moving off difficult to master. However, with plenty of practice, he will soon find moving off an easy manoeuvre. Tell the learner to take his time and not to put himself, "under a stop watch". When he has completed all the safety checks, you must show him the procedure for starting the engine. In the first lesson we referred to two additional safety checks that should be carried out (see figure 4). They are:

- Check the parking brake is on.
- Check the gear lever is in neutral.

They are two very important checks he must carry out every time he wishes to start the engine. If he starts the engine when the car is in a forward gear, the car will lurch forward and stall. The car should be positioned on a quiet road with no parked vehicles, gradients or bends. Keep your foot near to the dual brake (if you have one) and keep a good look out for traffic coming behind you. Never trust a learner. Always keep an eye on what he is doing as well as being aware of the general road and traffic situation, making full use of peripheral vision. Remember, it only takes a second for a traffic accident to occur (see figure 12).

Since moving off and making normal stops should normally be taught to a beginner (phase 1), you should give him a full instructional briefing highlighting the following key points:

- The importance of front and rear vision.
- The use of mirrors before moving off, signalling, changing direction, overtaking and braking.
- The correct Mirrors (Look, Assess, Decide), Signal, Manoeuvre routine.
- Moving away safely with proper use of the foot and hand controls.

- Stopping normally in a safe position with proper use of the foot and hand controls.

Before moving off, explain to the learner that you are going to teach him how to move off and stop. Give a simple and precise briefing. This will prepare him and he will be able to carry out your instructions without too much thought. With the vehicle stationary, permit the learner to practice changing gear, introduce the MSM routine and how to stop the car and make the vehicle safe. As soon as the learner moves off, you must talk him through each procedure step-by-step, in a calm, simple and unmistakable manner until he is ready to make decisions and take over the responsibility for his actions from yourself. If you stop giving instructions on the move, the learner may freeze and start to panic.

STOPPING SMOOTHLY
You should clearly instruct the learner how to stop the car. An example of this is as follows, *"Check your mirrors and signal if necessary. Position the car approximately 30 cm (1 foot) parallel from the kerb. Cover the brake, cover the clutch, gently brake, and when the car is at walking pace (about 5 mph), push the clutch down as fast as you can to stop the engine stalling. When the car is just about to stop, ease off the footbrake, apply the parking brake and select neutral. Take both feet off your pedals".*

Explain to the learner that the correct procedure he should carry out before moving off can be remembered by using the following code:

- **PREPARATION**
- **OBSERVATION**
- **MOVE**

To build up the learner's confidence and to ensure that first-time success is achieved, give the learner a full 'talk through' instruction using the preparation, observation, move routine.

Figure 12. Keep your eyes on the road.

The learner may check the mirrors and then look round before moving off but this does not mean that he took in what he saw. He may have looked for the sake of looking. This is known as "driving with blind eyes". You must assume full responsibility for the learner by making sure that he moves off safely with due regard for other road users (see figure 13). Many learners persistently move off when it is unsafe, even during the latter stages of the learning process. This is often attributed to lack of awareness of actual or potential danger or simply sheer inexperience. If a learner makes this mistake you must remind him of the dangers and consequences. However if the problem persists it is clear that you have not made the risks clear enough. Remember to treat the **cause**, not the effect. You must use tact and relate the fault to the potential financial loss.

Tell the learner to look over his right shoulder and to check the blind spot. In order to cross safely as a pedestrian, he has to correctly judge the speed and distance of any approaching traffic. Likewise, as a driver he should use similar judgement skills before moving away from the side of the road. In other words, if he was a pedestrian standing on the pavement, would he manage to walk across the road in time? If the answer is no, then he should not move off as a driver. In the section principles of instruction and methods of application, I recommended you to vary your methods of instruction to suit the learner's individual needs. On this occasion (as a last resort), you will have to stress the possibility of death and injury to himself and others. Although this may seem rather dramatic, learners must learn to face up to their responsibilities.

Figure 13. Don't forget to look over your shoulder and check your blind spot before moving off.

Some learners are anxious and get flustered before moving off, so it is very important that you keep your instructions short, simple and straight to the point. The idea is to encourage early success. If the learner succeeds in moving off and stopping safely you will boost his confidence. Be prepared for the clutch pedal coming up too high, erratic steering, and over-acceleration once the learner has moved off. Some learners panic when changing gear and try to apply the parking brake in desperation. Watch out for this so that you may take evasive action. If the learner experiences any difficulties, break the exercise down into component parts as this will help him understand things more easily (see figure 14).

You may have to give a practical demonstration to reinforce what you have already taught. If you give a practical demonstration make sure you take your time, and talk each stage through step-by-step, concentrating on the key points so that the learner will find it easier to understand. Everything may seem straightforward to you, but in the eyes of a learner driver simple things can appear rather complicated. Words to avoid are:

- "TOP GEAR" (sounds like stop here).
- "AND BRAKE" (sounds like hand brake).

Do not start an instruction with the words:

- "TURN" (the learner may turn without warning).
- "STOP" (except in an emergency).
- "RIGHT" (the learner may move or turn right without warning).

Figure 14. Before moving off or stopping, imagine that there is a glass of water on the bonnet of the car.

Encourage the learner from the outset to make progress to suit varying road and traffic conditions but within his own ability. Explain that other drivers get frustrated if they are held up unnecessarily and may take risks and overtake when unsafe. Remember, the classic way for effective teaching to a learner with limited experience (phase 1) can be remembered by using the following codes: **Explain, demonstrate, practice and validate**.

If the learner has difficulty in moving off due to bad clutch control, you should redress this immediately. Explain to the learner that there is free play in the clutch pedal and let him practice with his foot on the pedal to locate the holding point. Let the learner hold this for about three seconds and then allow him to creep forward for about 10 metres using the clutch, slipping where necessary. This is an excellent exercise to acquaint the learner with the clutch pedal, and teaches him how best to move off in a quick and efficient manner. This is the ideal time to introduce, *"Use the mirror, clutch down, gently brake to a stop"*. It is important that the learner uses the cup-hand/angled grip when changing gear (see figure 15).

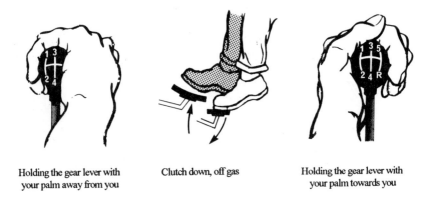

Holding the gear lever with   Clutch down, off gas   Holding the gear lever with
your palm away from you   your palm towards you

Figure 15. Holding the gear lever and changing gear.

It is highly important that the learner is totally familiarised with the Mirrors (Look, Assess, Decide), Signal, Manoeuvre routine, and that this is emphasised at every possible opportunity so that it becomes second nature. Ensure that the learner times the giving of a signal, taking into account the flow of traffic, but without undue hesitancy.

If the learner has difficulty in stopping at the correct place, give him "target practice" by selecting a roadside feature such as a lamp-post and train him to pull up level with the car's bumper. In the final stages of stopping, encourage peripheral vision which improves the steering rather than the learner concentrating on a nearby fixed point such as the kerb. Ensure that the learner uses progressive braking when stopping. It is also important that when the car has come to a standstill he keeps both feet on the pedals absolutely still, until the parking brake has been applied and the gear lever has been put into neutral. Ask the learner for a few examples of where it would be unsafe and illegal to stop. Ask your pupil to talk through the routine for moving off. This will encourage him to take over the responsibility from yourself.

Once the learner can move off and stop normally, drive to a long straight section of road (not on an incline), to practice the following braking and gear changing exercise. It is very important that the learner judges his braking to given situations on the road. Explain to the learner that braking is dependent on speed i.e. the faster the car is travelling, the **sooner** and not the harder, the brake should be applied. Braking should be gentle never severe. To give the learner practical experience the following example should be used (see figure 16). Ask the learner to drive along in fourth gear at 30 mph.

- 30 mph. Instruct the learner to make the decision to brake.
- 25 mph. Instruct the learner to change from fourth to third gear.
- 20 mph. Instruct the learner to analyse and adjust braking if necessary.
- 15 mph. Instruct the learner to change from third to second gear.
- 10 mph. Instruct the learner to analyse and adjust braking if necessary.
- 5 mph. Instruct the learner to change from second gear to first gear.
- <5 mph. Instruct the learner to gently brake and push the clutch down to stop the car. Once the car has come to a complete stop instruct the learner to apply the parking brake and select neutral.

Highlight the dangers of neutral being selected before the parking brake.

MOVING OFF UPHILL AND FROM BEHIND A PARKED VEHICLE

It is useful to permit the learner to let the car roll on the hill (either forwards or backwards depending on the slope). This lets the learner feel the effect of movement of the car and allows him to correct this with the clutch and to "hold" the car stationary. The learner should be taught that when moving off from behind another vehicle, he must be particularly careful to signal and observe properly. Due to the extra time the manoeuvre will take, the learner should be constantly vigilant because the road situation may have changed before he actually pulls off.

Stage 5	Stage 4	Stage 3	Stage 2	Stage 1
Clutch down gently	Select first gear	Select second gear	Select third gear	Travelling
brake to a stop - 5 mph	5 mph	15 mph	25 mph	at 30 mph

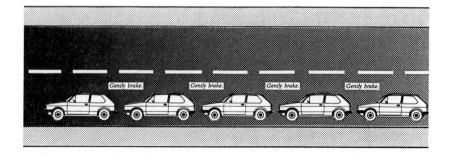

Figure 16. A braking and gear changing exercise.

MOVING OFF DOWNHILL

You should ensure that the learner knows the correct procedure for moving off downhill. To prevent the car from rolling forward down the gradient the learner **must** apply the footbrake before releasing the parking brake otherwise the car will move forward before he is fully prepared. The type of verbal instruction you give when the car is on the move is entirely at your own discretion. However, if you follow the correct procedure laid down in the, *'Principles of Instruction and Methods of Application'* (Chapter 1), the learner will find your instructions concise and simple to follow. If your instructions are too long winded, the learner will not have sufficient time to react to them.

Remember, the learner's car will cover a distance of 14 metres in one second if he is travelling at a speed of 30 mph. Therefore, give your instructions early and in a clear and unmistakeable manner as this will enable the learner to carry out all your commands in good time. If you fail to do this, the learner may panic, and you may be forced to activate the dual controls to avoid an accident.

SOME COMMON FAULTS COMMITTED BY LEARNERS: STEERING

- Steering with only one hand on the steering wheel unnecessarily.
- Incorrect or poor grip on the steering wheel.
- Erratic steering.
- Looking at the instructor or hand and foot controls whilst driving.
- Striking the kerb.
- Driving in the gutter.
- Poor forward observations.
- Staring intently at the bonnet, road ahead, kerb, parked vehicle or centre of the road whilst driving.
- Using one hand fixed on the steering wheel (like an anchor), whilst turning.
- Not using the "push and pull" method.
- Short non-fluid movements of the wheel.
- Excessive speed - the cause of many driving faults.

BEFORE AND AFTER STOPPING

- Not using the Mirrors (Look, Assess, Decide) routine well before stopping.
- Not stopping in a safe, legal or convenient place.
- Not stopping parallel or too far from the kerb.

- Harsh braking before stopping.
- Applying or grasping for the parking brake before the car comes to a complete stop.
- Stopping when unsafe to do so.
- Not de-clutching before stopping.
- De-clutching too early before stopping.
- De-clutching too late before stopping.
- Not realising the engine has stalled.
- Not applying the parking brake and selecting neutral (where necessary) after stopping.
- Removing the foot from the footbrake before applying the parking brake and selecting neutral.
- Failing to cancel the indicator signal after stopping.

Lesson 3 - Making proper use of the mirrors and giving signals

If the learner has never been taught how to make effective use of the mirrors (phase 1), you should give a full instructional briefing highlighting the following key points:

- The Mirrors (Look, Assess, Decide), Signal, Manoeuvre routine before making any driving decision.
- The limitations of the mirrors.
- The importance of rear vision.
- When and why the mirrors should be used before moving off, increasing speed, signalling, changing direction, overtaking, slowing down and stopping.

MIRRORS

Explain to the learner that the first thing he must do before he makes any driving decision is to check his mirrors. The mirrors are the eyes in the back of the head. Before deciding to give any signal, change direction, increase speed, slow down or stop, the mirrors must be checked well in advance. Late use of the mirrors will lead to poorly organised and hurried driving decisions. Stress to the learner that a good driver will always know what is behind and what is happening around the sides of the car.

Explain to the learner that effective use of mirrors means looking and acting sensibly on what was seen. In other words, he must **look**, **assess** and **decide** before making any driving decision. Discover if the learner knows how to adjust the mirrors in order to get the best all-round vision with the least amount of head movement; quiz the learner about blind spots. Relate the use of mirrors to the Mirrors (Look, Assess, Decide) routine in order to establish that the learner's actions will be safe to perform.

It is crucially important that the learner always looks round before moving off. However, some learner drivers don't really understand where the blind spot actually is, so they tend to look round simply for the sake of it. You must watch out for this and educate them accordingly. Make sure the learner does not just give a superficial look round before moving off. Ensure the learner turns the head and torso well round and stress the dangers and consequences of not checking the blind spot. Explain to the learner that the mirrors must be checked **regularly**, to confirm what is happening behind and to the sides of his vehicle.

THE BLIND SPOT

A useful exercise in appreciating the mirrors' limitations is to park at the left-hand side of the road and then watch for a slow moving vehicle appearing in the right-hand mirror. Follow its progress and when the vehicle disappears in this mirror, that is the blind spot.

When the learner is driving you should assist him verbally and take full responsibility as to when it is safe to change direction, slow down, or stop. The learner will gain experience and confidence in the use of mirrors with plenty of driving practice and build up his own judgement as to when it is safe to change direction. It is also important to encourage the learner to use a systematic scanning method (see figure 17). For example:

Look well ahead - check main mirror - look well ahead - check right-hand mirror - look well ahead - check speed.

DUAL EYE MIRRORS

The instructor's rear view mirror(s) should be correctly adjusted to give maximum vision with minimum movement. They will also help you to see what is happening behind and to the sides of your vehicle. The dual eye mirror, strategically placed and focused on the learner's eyes, will enable you to check that the learner is making **effective** use of the mirrors.

SOME COMMON FAULTS COMMITTED BY LEARNERS:
MIRRORS

- Not using the Mirrors (Look, Assess, Decide), Signal, Manoeuvre routine.
- Failing to check the mirrors before moving off, increasing speed, signalling, changing direction, slowing down or stopping.
- Not making effective use of mirrors or failing to act sensibly on what was seen in the mirrors.
- Late use of the mirrors.
- Staring intently at the mirror.
- Failing to check the mirrors during normal driving.
- Offsetting the mirror(s) in order to make an excessive head movement.

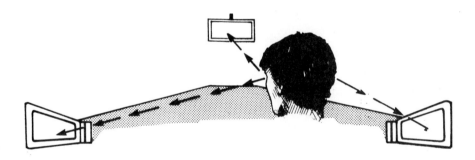

Figure 17. Make effective use of mirrors before making a driving decision.

Chapter 3

Lesson 4 - Approaching and turning corners

As soon as the learner has mastered the basics of driving, you should teach him a uniform and methodical system of car control. The system of car control he should use before he makes any driving decision is Mirrors (look, Assess, Decide), Signal, Manoeuvre, Position, Speed and Look (M.S.M.P.S.L.). Get the learner into the habit of using this system and tell him to learn it by heart because he will be using it many times whilst driving.

Explain to the learner that a corner is where two roads meet - it is also known as a road junction. Some corners are very sharp and some are just simply bends in the road. He must always remember that once he has decided to turn into the corner, the speed of his car must be completely under control and he must maintain the same speed throughout the corner. Accelerating into a corner too quickly is a dangerous practice. If the speed is not under complete control he may cause the car to skid or he may drive 'blind' into some danger without having time to brake. The important thing to remember is that, *the sharper the corner, the slower his speed must be; the slower his speed, the lower the gear; the lower the gear, the more control he will have.*

Approaching and turning corners should normally be taught to a learner who is already comfortable and confident with the basic controls of the car. If the learner has never been taught how to approach and turn corners (phase 1), you should give a full briefing, highlighting the following key points:

- Making proper use of mirrors, signals, brakes and gears when approaching the corner.
- Not coasting on approach or whilst turning the corner.
- Avoiding excessive or crawling speeds on the approach or whilst turning the corner.
- Correct line of approach and position on turning.
- Give way to pedestrians who are crossing at or near junctions.
- Not turning in front of traffic closely approaching from the opposite direction when making a right turn.
- The dangers and avoidance of cutting right-hand corners.
- Proper observations into side road/waiting before point of turn.

Use diagrams so that the learner will understand what you are describing. If the learner has limited experience, talk him through this exercise stage-by-stage, repeating the Mirrors, Signal, Position, Speed and Look routine until he can do it competently. With plenty of practice, approaching and turning corners will eventually become second nature. Permit the learner to talk himself through the routine for approaching and turning corners.

SPEED
Highlight the importance of approaching corners at the correct speed - not so fast as to lose control, but not so slow that it could hold up other road users. You should instruct the learner to slow down with the footbrake to approximately 10 mph (if necessary) and change directly from fourth gear into second gear. Second gear should be selected approximately 10 metres (3 car lengths) from the corner. The clutch at this point must be brought fully up, which will assist him in braking and help to slow down the car. The speed and gear the learner should use will depend on the angle of the corner and field of vision. You may have to give a practical demonstration on how to approach and turn corners to reinforce what you have already taught. You should get into the habit of telling a learner what to do. Telling a

learner what **not** to do should be avoided because this is negative thinking (see figure 18).

An important point you must get across is that the sequence of changing down the gears is not paramount, but the speed must be under the learner's control. When the learner has grasped the basics, you can allow him to try it without any verbal assistance. Although the Mirrors, Signal, Manoeuvre routine is very important you must emphasise the Mirrors, Signal, Brake and Gears routine in simple detail. Encourage the learner to repeat the Mirrors, Signal, Manoeuvre routine out loud whilst approaching and turning corners. This will enable you to find out exactly where any weaknesses lie and what mistakes he is making during the exercise.

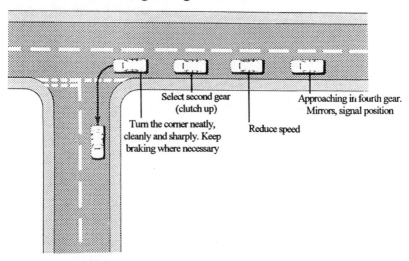

Select second gear
(clutch up)

Approaching in fourth gear.
Mirrors, signal position

Turn the corner neatly,
cleanly and sharply. Keep
braking where necessary

Reduce speed

Figure 18. Approaching and turning a corner to the left.

TURNING RIGHT

Explain to the learner that turning right is potentially hazardous since it may involve crossing the path of oncoming vehicles and the learner must also be mindful of pedestrians crossing the road. Turning right is far more difficult than turning left and there are slight variations. Again, apply the Mirrors (Look, Assess, Decide), Signal, Manoeuvre,

Position, Speed and Look routine. You should tell the learner to position the car approximately 30 cm (1 foot) from the centre of the road. However, the learner should keep well into the left if turning right out of a narrow road (this is to allow room for other vehicles to turn in) whilst increasing his vision into the new road. If the learner is travelling in a one-way street, the vehicle should be positioned according to whether he intends to turn right or left. If the learner wishes to turn right, he should keep to the right-hand lane as long as there are no parked vehicles or obstructions on the right-hand side of the road. On the other hand, if the learner wants to turn left, the vehicle should be positioned in the left-hand lane.

You should also encourage the learner to start looking early into the side roads when approaching corners, so that he can act sensibly if he sees any signs of danger. Point out the specific dangers he may come across and explain how to deal with them. Emphasise the need for a final check in the offside mirror for any overtaking traffic. Stress the dangers of cutting in front of traffic closely approaching from the opposite direction whilst making a right turn. The best way for the learner to judge if it is safe to turn is to ask himself, *"Is there any possibility that I may make the oncoming vehicle slow down or alter course?"* If the answer is *yes*, then he must wait. On the other hand if the answer is *no*, then he may turn in front of the other vehicle. Finally, discourage driving too close to the kerb, crossing the centre of the road or cutting right-hand corners (see figures 19 and 20).

Make sure you give your instructions in good time and in a clear and unmistakable manner. If the learner can approach and turn corners successfully he will be ready to learn how to approach and deal with road junctions. When the learner has reached test standard (phase 2), you should double check his method of turning corners to ensure he is still following the correct procedure. You may have to correct any errors made by the learner on the move, but get to the root of any faults if any driving errors are repeated. Some instructors prefer to teach turning right first before moving on, to show the differences in relation to turning left.

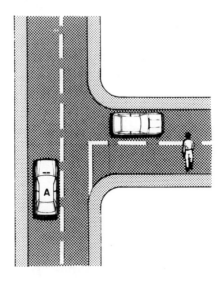

Figure 19. Always look into a new road before turning.

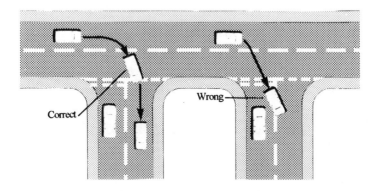

Figure 20. Avoid cutting corners.

It should be noted that many learner drivers (especially women), will experience great difficulty in distinguishing "left" from "right" due to a psychological condition known as Gerstmann's syndrome. This is very difficult to correct, and can be problematic since the learner's response time will be much longer as they must mentally work out which side is which, rather than being a "reflex" action. Nevertheless, the instructor must still use the terminology of "right" and "left" (rather than hand directions, etc.) as this is the terminology which will be used by the examiner in the driving test.

SOME COMMON FAULTS COMMITTED BY LEARNERS: APPROACHING AND TURNING CORNERS

- Not using the Mirrors (Look, Assess, Decide), Signal, Manoeuvre routine.
- Not acting properly on information received from the mirrors.
- Giving an incorrect or misleading signal/failing to cancel the signal.
- Not positioning the car correctly either before or after turning.
- Not reducing speed sufficiently before turning the corner/cutting the corner.
- Selecting a low gear at an excessive speed or the wrong gear.
- Poor co-ordination whilst braking and changing gear.
- Looking down when changing gear or changing gear too late.
- Turning the corner with the clutch held down.
- Oversteering, understeering, failing to keep the correct course before turning and failing to straighten up after turning.
- Letting the car move forward past the turning point, resulting in a "hook" turn.
- Not giving way to pedestrians crossing the road - before or whilst turning.
- Not looking early into the side roads on the approach.
- Failing to anticipate the actions of pedestrians and other drivers or stopping needlessly.
- Not using the "push and pull" method whilst turning.
- Turning in front of closely approaching traffic when turning right.

Lesson 5 - Dealing with road junctions

Once the learner has mastered how to approach and turn corners, you should move on and teach him how to deal with more complex road junctions. Explain that there are many different kinds of road junction. One essential fact to be remembered is that all road junctions are dangerous irrespective of whether or not he has priority. Therefore, he should never become complacent. Dealing with road junctions should normally be taught to a learner who is partly trained and can approach and turn corners to a competent standard. If the learner has never been taught how to deal with road junctions (phase 1), give a full instructional briefing, highlighting the following key points:

- Mirrors (Look, Assess, Decide), Signal, Manoeuvre routine.
- Use of mirrors, signals, brakes, and gears.
- Avoidance of excessive speed or crawling on the approach.
- Correct line on approach or whilst turning.
- Give way to pedestrians before turning.
- Not coasting on the approach or while turning.
- Proper judgement of speed and distance of other vehicles.
- Emerging with due regard for other road users.

You may have to give a practical demonstration on how to approach give way junctions at the correct speed and further demonstrate how and where to change through the gears. Talk each movement through with the learner to develop a smooth and planned approach with good observations. It is important that when you give your instructions this is done in good time and in a clear and unmistakable manner. As soon as the learner can deal with road junctions competently allow him to practice without any verbal assistance.

Give your instructions at least 92 metres (100 yards) before the give way junction. Give the learner plenty of time and do not rush him. Make sure that the learner brings the clutch up between each gear change, otherwise he will be **coasting** and this is a very difficult habit to break. When practicing road junctions at the early stages in the learning process, instruct the learner to stop at the junction. This will give you and the learner sufficient time to take effective observation before emerging.

When waiting at a give way junction for a safe gap in the traffic, instruct the learner to be patient in giving way to other vehicles, pedestrians and cyclists on the main road. If the learner still has limited experience and his judgement is poor, you must take full responsibility and tell him when it is safe to emerge from the junction. Explain to the learner that parts of the car can obstruct his vision and he must take this into account at all times. Learners often find it difficult to judge other driver's speed and distance so you should encourage him to build up a safe judgement of when to emerge into a main road. Tell the learner to watch out for any vehicles or cyclists that may be emerging from a side road or driveway, because they may be hidden by parked vehicles or roadside furniture.

Emphasise that the gears **assist** the car to slow down and that they are used in conjunction with the footbrake. Using the gears without braking could mean that other drivers will not know that the learner is slowing down because the brake lights will not illuminate. If practicing this procedure for the first time it would be prudent to keep your right foot near the dual brake during the manoeuvre as the learner may "freeze" and so not stop at the give way lines.

When the learner's driving develops, encourage him to avoid stopping, but only if it is safe to proceed at give way junctions. The principle gear taken when emerging from the give way junction should match the speed and this should match the visibility. Point out the dangers of stopping needlessly. Tell the learner that other drivers may take risks and overtake when it is unsafe if they are inconvenienced at give way junctions. To avoid undue hesitancy you must encourage him to creep slowly forward until the zone of visibility opens up (see figure 21) so that he may observe properly before making a decision to move into the new road. Ask the following questions to ensure that the learner is looking;

- *"Can you see beyond the parked vehicle?"*
- *" Is it clear?"*
- *"Can you see any pedestrians?"*

As the learner's skill progresses, more complex junctions should be introduced which require greater control and effective observation skills.

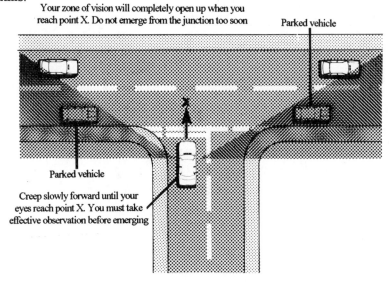

Figure 21. Effective observation before emerging.

TO SUM UP

A word of warning. Never allow a learner to emerge from any give way junction if he sees another driver signalling his intention to turn. It is prudent to wait until he receives more positive information before emerging, i.e. wait until the other driver slows down and makes a definite move to turn. The other driver may have left his indicator on by mistake. There is one crucial rule regarding give way junctions. If the learner is in any doubt and his vision is restricted in any way, he must **STOP** and not emerge from the give way junction until he is quite sure it is safe to do so. Remember, *"If in doubt - DON'T".*

Lesson 6 - Dealing with crossroads

Explain to the learner that a road which crosses the path of another road is called a crossroad. There are many different types of crossroads. It is important to remember that **all** crossroads are dangerous and they must be treated with caution. Although the learner may have priority there is nothing to stop a vehicle or cyclist pulling straight out. Stress that he must **always** take effective observation before emerging. If the learner has never been taught how to deal with crossroads (phase 1), you should give a full instructional briefing, highlighting the following key points:

- Use the Mirrors (Look, Assess, Decide), Signal, Manoeuvre routine.
- Correct regulation of speed and gears on the approach.
- Not coasting on the approach or whilst turning.
- Taking effective observation **before** emerging.
- Emerging with due regard for other road users.
- Position the car correctly before and after turning right and left.
- Giving way to pedestrians before and whilst turning.
- Correctly judge other driver's speed before turning in front of traffic closely approaching from the opposite direction when making a right turn.
- The danger and avoidance of cutting right-hand corners.

Take the learner to areas where he will experience various types of crossroads, especially crossroads which are unmarked. During the initial lessons, talk each stage through to the learner of the Mirrors (Look, Assess, Decide), Signal, Manoeuvre, Position, Speed and Look routine in a simple straightforward way. By using the 'question and answer technique' you can build on the learner's experience with that which he has already learnt when dealing with road junctions. You should be able to gauge at what stage the learner is ready to take over the responsibility for his actions and decisions from yourself. A useful exercise is to stop the car some distance from an uncontrolled crossroad and emphasise to the learner where he should start to look early (see figure 22).

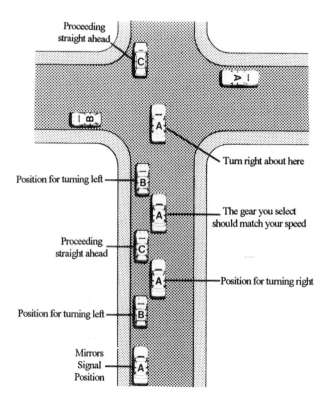

Figure 22. Dealing with an uncontrolled crossroad.

Point out where the learner should start taking effective observation before emerging and further indicate where he should keep going ("point of no return") at the intersection, if a vehicle emerges. The learner must also be told where to accelerate out of trouble to clear the hazard in the shortest possible time.

Whilst checking the crossroad, many learners have a tendency to let their steering wander, especially when proceeding straight on. You must watch out for this and draw it to the attention of the learner should you see it happening. If the steering problem re-occurs you should get the learner to give quick glances to the right (avoid staring) left and right. Since most of his concentration will be focused on the road, you must not allow the learner to get away with just superficial head movements.

If you need to give a lengthy explanation, instruct the pupil to stop at the side of the road. When giving the briefing you should show pictures or draw diagrams which will assist him in understanding what is being taught. Explain how the learner should respond if there is a vehicle waiting to emerge from the opposite junction.

Turning right at crossroads is one of the most difficult and hazardous manoeuvres for the learner because of oncoming traffic. Therefore you and the learner should be particularly careful and observant during this exercise. Encourage the learner always to have respect for crossing pedestrians and give way to them where necessary. Tell the learner **where** to look, **what** to look out for, and **how** to react to actual and potential danger at crossroads. It is very important that the learner understands the rules governing offside to offside and nearside to nearside when meeting other traffic at crossroads. It is crucial that you develop the learners awareness of the very real risks when dealing with crossroads (see figures 23 and 24).

ADVANTAGES AND DISADVANTAGES

Explain to the learner the advantage of turning nearside to nearside is that his vision is not restricted into the road into which he is turning. The advantage of turning offside to offside is that he can see traffic hidden behind the oncoming vehicle. The disadvantage of turning nearside to nearside is that he may find it difficult to see traffic hidden behind the oncoming vehicle. The disadvantage of turning offside to offside is that other vehicles can block the learner's vision into his new road. Sometimes road markings will guide him in which way to turn, so the learner must act accordingly.

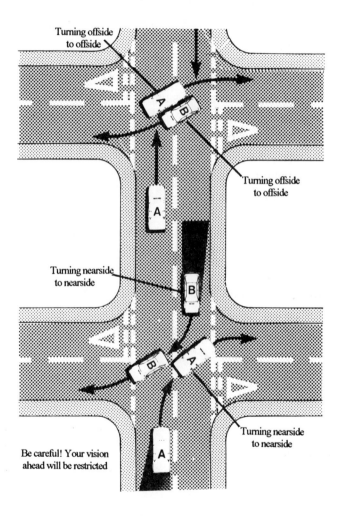

Figure 23. Turning offside to offside at a major crossroad.
Figure 24. Turning nearside to nearside at a major crossroad.

SOME COMMON FAULTS COMMITTED BY LEARNERS: JUNCTIONS AND CROSSROADS

- Not using the Mirrors (Look, Assess, Decide), Signal, Manoeuvre routine.
- Not complying with a mandatory "Stop" sign/road marking.
- Not regulating speed correctly on the approach.
- Not taking effective observation before emerging.
- Not judging the speed and distance of other traffic and emerging when unsafe.
- Stopping with the front of the car past the kerbline of the junction when unsafe.
- Not positioning the car correctly before or after turning.
- Emerging from the junction in the wrong gear.
- Cutting the corner.
- Failing to give way to pedestrians who are crossing the road.
- Not taking effective observation when dealing with a minor or major crossroad.
- Not emerging from the junction when a suitable gap appears.
- Not anticipating the actions of other road users.
- Turning in front of closely approaching traffic when turning right.

Chapter 4

Lesson 7 - Reversing in a straight line

Reversing in a straight line should be taught to a learner before he is shown more complicated manoeuvres (phase 1). The road you select must be as flat as possible. Keep away from bends, parked vehicles, road junctions etc., as this will allow the learner to carry out the exercise without any distractions. The learner should be instructed to aim the eyes high along the road to the rear of the car, and to rely on peripheral vision when reversing. If the learner does not have a comfortable seating position he will find this exercise difficult to perform - he may release the seatbelt for ease of movement. Inform the learner that he can modify the basic holding position by using his right hand only at the 12 o'clock position. Whilst reversing in a straight line he can place his left hand on the back of the passenger seat.

You should partially assist the learner with steering if any difficulties arise and the exercise should be repeated until the learner is able to perform it successfully without any verbal or physical assistance. If the learner can reverse in a straight line competently, he will find the turn in the road, reversing into a limited opening and parking between two vehicles easier to perform and understand.

Many learner drivers wrongly imagine that in reverse gear the car travels the opposite way to that in which he turns the steering wheel. Initially, emphasise the importance of low speed control and when this skill improves, encourage the learner to look out for other road users and to be prepared to give way to them where necessary. In the correct terminology when reversing, the steering wheel should be turned, "towards or away from the kerb" **not** "left or right". There are particular risks associated with this exercise (e.g. failing to give way to other road users or steering dangerously off-course) and these risks should be clearly pointed out to the learner (see figure 25). A very important point to tell the learner is that when the car is driven forwards he can see the car turning with the steering. However, whilst reversing, he will have to wait for the steering to take effect. Instruct the learner to use the preparation, observation, move routine before moving off.

Figure 25. Reversing in a straight line.

Lesson 8 - Turning round using forward and reverse gears

The turn in the road can be taught soon after the learner can move off at an angle (phase 1) and can competently reverse in a straight line. These form the basic skills required for this manoeuvre. Explain to the learner that the idea of this manoeuvre is for him to turn his car round to face the opposite direction using forward and reverse gears, under control and with due regard for other road users.

Explain to the learner the reason for this manoeuvre is to show the examiner that he can use and co-ordinate all the major controls of the car within a limited space (i.e. the space between the two kerb stones). When the learner is sitting the driving test it is essential that he does not touch the kerb stones during this manoeuvre. Explain that this is a helpful exercise if there are no side roads for the car to reverse into.

Before commencing the turn in the road he must ask himself, *"Is it safe? Is it legal? Is it convenient?"* Tell the learner that he must look at the 'camber' of the road so that he will be able to judge how much power the car will need for the manoeuvre. The best way to teach this exercise is to split the manoeuvre into three stages.

Initially, you should encourage low-speed control whilst personally keeping a look out for other vehicles and pedestrians. You must take full responsibility for the safety of other road users when this exercise is being carried out. You should be able to gauge at what stage the learner is ready to take over the responsibility for his actions and decisions from yourself. If the learner has never been taught how to turn the car round using forward and reverse gears (phase 1) you should give a full instructional briefing followed by a practical demonstration on each movement of the three stages, with the emphasis on low speed control.

The following are the key points to relay to the learner:

- Co-ordination of the major controls with the steering.
- Observations just before and whilst turning.
- Being reasonably accurate in positioning.
- Select a legal, safe and convenient place for the manoeuvre.

The road you select must be as flat as possible. Keep your car away from bends, parked vehicles, road junctions etc. In other words give the learner plenty of room. If your car can be turned round in one movement, then the road is too wide.

Initially, teach the learner to turn the car round on level ground in order that he may control the car more easily. Explain to the learner that he must co-ordinate the use of the foot and hand controls so that he can move the car smoothly and accurately. Later when his skills improve, progress to narrow roads with steeper cambers so that he may practice turning round in these conditions. Explain the value of the exercise and the reason why the manoeuvre should be executed competently. The idea is to encourage early success. If the learner succeeds at the first attempt it will boost confidence enormously (see figure 26).

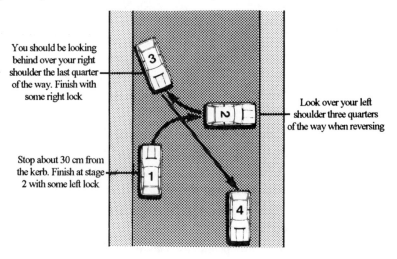

You should be looking behind over your right shoulder the last quarter of the way. Finish with some right lock

Look over your left shoulder three quarters of the way when reversing

Stop about 30 cm from the kerb. Finish at stage 2 with some left lock

Figure 26. Turning round using forward and reverse gears.

If the learner experiences any difficulty performing the manoeuvre do not be over-critical. Reassure him that difficulty in the early stages is quite common and it could take many attempts before it becomes second nature. Learners tend to panic when they see another vehicle approaching. If other road users are present in the distance the learner should be encouraged to carry on. However, you should instruct him to give priority to other road users if they are nearby. Under no circumstances let him rush the manoeuvre. Remember the rule: *"Keep the feet slow and move the hands fast".*

There are particular risks associated with this manoeuvre such as pedestrians appearing from a blind spot, fast moving vehicles which the learner fails to notice, etc. These risks should be clearly pointed out. It is therefore crucial that the learner keeps looking out of the rear window as much as possible. The learner must know how to handle the situation, if traffic or any other danger approaches whilst he is carrying out the manoeuvre.

**SOME COMMON FAULTS COMMITTED BY LEARNERS:
TURNING IN THE ROAD**
- Not co-ordinating the accelerator, footbrake, clutch or parking brake with steering.
- Stalling the engine due to poor co-ordination.
- Striking the kerb or mounting the pavement.
- Not observing properly before and during the manoeuvre.
- Turning the steering wheel too slowly and not achieving reasonable accuracy.
- Not acting properly when other road users arrive.
- Turning the car round using too many movements.
- Turning the steering wheel the wrong way.
- Failing to release the parking brake.
- Stopping needlessly.
- Not giving way to other vehicles and pedestrians.

Lesson 9 - Reversing to the left

Reversing around a corner can be taught before commencing with a turn in the road. It makes no difference as long as the learner can reverse competently in a straight line. If the learner has never been taught reversing to the left (phase 1), you should give a full instructional briefing, highlighting the following key points:

- Select a safe, legal and convenient place for the manoeuvre.
- Co-ordination of the controls with the steering.
- Observations just before and whilst turning.
- Being reasonably accurate in positioning.
- Act properly to the presence and actions of other road users.

You must watch carefully that the learner observes into the side road, and carries out the Mirrors (Look, Assess, Decide) Signal, Manoeuvre routine when stopping - position the car correctly before carrying out the manoeuvre. Explain the value of the exercise and the reasons why the manoeuvre should be executed competently. Before attempting the exercise the learner should again ask himself, *"Is it safe? Is it legal? Is it convenient?"* Initially, concentrate on low-speed control whilst personally keeping a look out for other vehicles and pedestrians. Explain to the learner that he must co-ordinate the use of the foot and hand controls so that he can move the car smoothly and accurately. Later you should gauge when the learner is capable of taking over this responsibility. The learner must be made aware that the front of the car will swing out when the rear of the car turns into the corner. At this point, the learner should look over his right shoulder to check the blind spot. The learner must also know how to handle the situation if traffic or any other danger approaches whilst carrying out the manoeuvre.

As soon as the learner can see that the kerb has disappeared in the rear window, he should follow the kerb round. Tell the learner to imagine the position of the rear nearside wheel, just behind the back seat, to the edge of the kerb, and keep that wheel parallel to the kerb. He must turn the steering wheel sufficiently to get the car round the corner. The sharper the corner, the more the learner will have to turn the wheel to get the car round. Encourage the learner to, *"Keep the feet slow and move the hands fast"*. Remember that the examiner is not interested in how close the learner can get to the kerb, but rather in the overall control and observations throughout the manoeuvre.

Encourage the learner to perform the exercise in one complete movement. Do not worry if the learner finishes the exercise well away from the kerb. This is quite common in the early stages, and you should be more concerned about the observations and control displayed by the learner during the manoeuvre. With plenty of practice the learner will eventually finish close and parallel to the kerb. It is a popular misconception that a learner will fail the test if he does not keep and finish very close to the kerb. In fact, if the learner gets too close to the kerb, there is a possibility that he may strike it, the camber could drag the vehicle into the kerb or may run over any debris lying in the gutter (see figure 27).

The learner may have a tendency to look forward whilst reversing. If he takes his eyes from the back of the car, he may lose his sense of direction and the car will wander all over the road. The only time the learner should look forward is to check for other road users approaching the front of the car. However, it only takes a second for a pedestrian to walk behind the car. It is therefore imperative that the learner keeps looking out the rear window as much as possible.

Often, after the reverse has been completed, the learner will be thinking how well or badly he has carried out the reverse and may forget to check the mirrors and blind spot before moving off. This can be dangerous for obvious reasons, but you should ensure he does not drive off without first checking the mirrors, and looking round for traffic and pedestrians in the blind spot.

Initially, teach learners to reverse on level ground so that they may more easily control the car, and to ensure reasonable success to build up their confidence. Later, allow them to progress onto up and downhill gradients so that they may practice reversing in these conditions. There are particular risks associated with this manoeuvre. For example, steering dangerously off-course and failing to give way to other road users are risks which should be clearly pointed out.

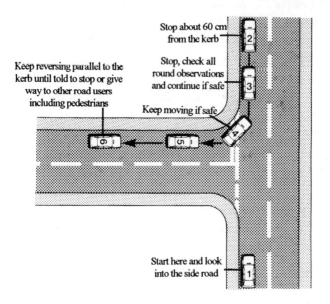

Stop about 60 cm from the kerb

Stop, check all round observations and continue if safe

Keep reversing parallel to the kerb until told to stop or give way to other road users including pedestrians

Keep moving if safe

Start here and look into the side road

Figure 27. Reversing around a corner to the left.

SOME COMMON FAULTS COMMITTED BY LEARNERS: REVERSING AROUND A CORNER

- Failing to check into the side road when driving past the corner.
- Not adopting the correct position prior to reversing.
- Reversing too fast and failing to keep full control of the clutch.
- Stalling the engine.
- Not observing properly before and during the manoeuvre.
- Not giving way to other vehicles and pedestrians.
- Striking the kerb or mounting the pavement.
- Not acting properly when other road users arrive.
- Reversing around the corner too widely or not correcting in time.

Lesson 10 - Reversing to the right

This topic can be taught to a learner who is both competent at turning a car round using forward and reverse gears, and reversing into a limited opening to the left. If the learner has never been taught how to reverse to the right (phase 1), you should give a full instructional briefing, highlighting the following key points:

- Select a legal, safe and convenient place for the manoeuvre.
- Co-ordination of the accelerator, footbrake, clutch, parking brake with the steering.
- Observations just before and whilst turning.
- Being reasonably accurate in positioning.
- Respond correctly to the presence and actions of others.

Explain the value of the exercise and why the manoeuvre should be executed competently. You must watch carefully that the learner observes into the side road, uses the Mirror (Look, Assess, Decide) Signal, Manoeuvre routine when stopping and that he positions the car correctly before carrying out the manoeuvre (see figure 28).

Instruct the learner to look over his left shoulder out of the rear window. If it is safe, he should reverse slowly under full control, slipping the clutch as necessary. Occasionally looking forward and checking for oncoming traffic. As soon as the learner reaches the point of turn, he should check ahead because when he starts to steer, the front of the car will swing out. At this point the learner should also check over his right shoulder and look at the road into which he is going to reverse. As soon as it is safe (make a final check over the left shoulder) the learner should keep looking over the right shoulder and continue reversing slowly, using clutch control and follow the kerb around. As the car becomes almost parallel again, the learner should look over his left shoulder to look out of the rear window, and straighten up the wheels.

The learner should continue to reverse (keep looking out of the rear window) in a straight line keeping reasonably close to the kerb, for at least 4-5 car lengths (conditions permitting) from the junction and then gently brake to a stop. The learner should then apply the parking brake and select neutral. The learner reverses so far back so that he will be well away from the junction, and in a safer position before moving off again. Before moving off, the learner must check over his left shoulder, as the blind spot on this occasion is on the left-hand side. When he drives off, the learner should move over to the correct side of the road before getting to the junction.

There are particular risks associated with this manoeuvre such as the front of the car swinging out whilst reversing and the movement of other road users. These risks should be clearly pointed out to the learner, who should be constantly vigilant throughout the exercise. Do not be surprised if the learner cannot perfect this exercise first time. He may need plenty of practice until he is successful. Initially, teach the learner to reverse to the right on level ground to ensure early success. Later, practice reversing to the right, on up and downhill gradients. The learner must know how to handle the situation if traffic or any other danger approaches whilst performing this manoeuvre.

SOME COMMON FAULTS COMMITTED BY LEARNERS: REVERSING AROUND A CORNER

- Not using the Mirrors (Look, Assess, Decide) Signal, Manoeuvre routine before stopping.
- Failing to check into the side road when driving past the corner.
- Not adopting the correct position prior to reversing.
- Reversing too fast.
- Failing to keep full control of the clutch.
- Stalling the engine.
- Not observing properly before and during the manoeuvre.
- Not giving way to other vehicles and pedestrians.
- Striking the kerb or mounting the pavement.

- Not acting properly when other road users arrive.
- Reversing around the corner too widely or not correcting in time.
- Turning the steering wheel too early.
- Stopping needlessly.

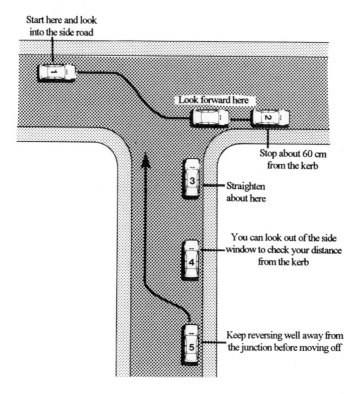

Figure 28. Reversing around a corner to the right.

Lesson 11 - Reverse parking

Reverse parking should be the final manoeuvre taught to the learner. If the learner has never been taught how to park between two vehicles (phase 1), give a full instructional briefing, highlighting the following:

- Select a legal, safe and convenient place for the exercise.
- Co-ordination of the major controls and steering to achieve reasonable accuracy.
- Observations before and throughout the exercise.
- Responding correctly to presence of other road users including pedestrians.

To successfully accomplish this manoeuvre, instruct the learner to drive forward, apply the Mirrors (Look, Assess, Decide) Signal, Manoeuvre routine and position the car level or slightly ahead of the first vehicle and parallel to it. Make sure that he is approximately 90 cm (3 feet) away from the side of this vehicle. Tell the learner he may release the seatbelt for ease of movement if he wishes, and to carry out the Preparation, Observation, Move routine.

Make sure that the learner turns well round in the seat and reverses back slowly, turning the steering wheel slightly to the left. The learner should attempt to place the left part (driver's side) of the rear window at the front nearside (passenger's side) headlight of the parked vehicle. At this point, the learner should check over his right shoulder to check the blind spot. When the front of the car has cleared the rear of the forward parked vehicle, tell him to turn the steering wheel quickly to the right. Continue reversing and when the car is nearly straight, steer left to straighten the front wheels.

Although it may seem obvious, it should be explained that more space is required in simply driving a car in a forward direction into a space at the side of the road, than in reverse parking using reverse gear (hence the need for the latter manoeuvre) (see figure 29).

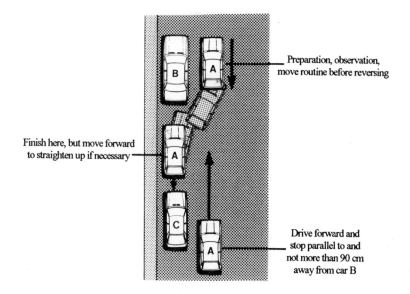

Preparation, observation, move routine before reversing

Finish here, but move forward to straighten up if necessary

Drive forward and stop parallel to and not more than 90 cm away from car B

Figure 29. Reverse parking.

To build up confidence, initially teach the learner to reverse park using only one parked car. When he has mastered the technique, teach the learner to park with the vehicles 2 or 3 car lengths apart so that he may perform the manoeuvre successfully. Later, allow him to practice with the vehicles closer together (1½ car lengths).

There are particular risks associated with this exercise, for example, striking the other vehicle and swinging the car out in the path of oncoming vehicles. Ask the learner three places where this exercise should not be carried out (e.g. one way streets). Emphasise the advantages of low-speed control and awareness of other road users. Inform the learner that if he is causing any inconvenience to other road users whilst reversing, he should pause until it is safe to continue. Explain the value of the exercise, and the reason why the manoeuvre should be executed competently. If another vehicle stops close behind you, move on and practice parking somewhere else.

Chapter 5

Lesson 12 - Judging speed, making progress and general road positioning

If the learner has never been taught how to exercise proper care in the use of speed (phase 1), you should give a full instructional briefing, highlighting the dangers and avoidance of excessive speed for the conditions. Ask the learner questions to establish what he knows about the varying speed limits and how these should be related to the road and traffic conditions.

EXERCISING PROPER CARE IN THE USE OF SPEED
It is a popular misconception that if a learner on a driving test has failed because of speeding, the speed limit has been broken. Of course this is possible, but it could also be that during the driving test, in the examiner's opinion, the learner was driving too fast for the conditions at the time. A possible example might be the learner passing a school at 30 mph with children running riot on the pavement. The examiner may fail him because of this - a more appropriate speed may be 20 or possibly 10 mph. Stress to the learner that he must always build up a judgement of what is **safe**, not necessarily what is legal.

A SAFE SPEED
Explain that speed is far and away the most common cause of death on the roads. A safe speed is one at which the driver can stop under full control in a safe position on the road, well within the distance seen to be clear. Explain that different types of weather conditions, the state of the road and any hazards on the road, will affect the speed

of his car. The learner should slow down, and make sure he can stop safely, well within the distance seen to be clear. If travelling on any roads outside built-up areas it does not mean he can go as fast as he wishes. The learner must obey the speed limit for the road he is travelling on and the rules laid down in the Highway Code. Inform the learner that he must never accelerate into any hazard and be prepared to select a lower gear as the situation demands.

It is difficult to give a practical demonstration to a learner about the proper care in the use of speed. However, you should explain to the learner about the two second rule as laid down in the Highway Code. Quiz him about stopping distances and ensure that he converts this into reality. The overall stopping distance may only be a figure in his head (see figure 30).

mph	THINKING DISTANCE		BRAKING DISTANCE		OVERALL STOPPING DISTANCE	
	m	*ft*	*m*	*ft*	*m*	*ft*
20	6	20	6	20	12	40
30	9	30	14	45	23	75
40	12	40	24	80	36	120
50	15	50	38	125	53	175
60	18	60	55	180	73	240
70	21	70	75	245	96	315

Figure 30. Shortest stopping distances.

It is imperative that you ensure the learner does not drive too quickly. This is dangerous for obvious reasons, but you should also explain to the learner that if he is moving along the road at too great a speed, he will most probably suffer from "information overload" and be unable to deal with any hazards, should they suddenly emerge.

If the learner has difficulty in judging speeds, park at the side of the road so that he may observe other traffic moving to visualise their speeds. Excessive speed often results from incorrect attitudes; lack of awareness of actual or potential danger. Try to isolate and deal with the problem of speeding in a logical way by treating the **cause** of the fault rather than its effect. The learner may not appreciate the dangers of driving too fast as he may either have a poor perception of speed or is a frequent passenger in a fast-driven car (see figure 31).

Figure 31. You must exercise proper care in the use of speed.

If the learner persistently drives too fast for the road conditions, stop the side of the road and explain the consequences and dangers of this type of driving. Explain also that if he continually drives too fast during his driving test the driving examiner may terminate the test in the interests of public safety.

SOME COMMON FAULTS COMMITTED BY LEARNERS: CARE IN THE USE OF SPEED

- Driving too fast for the prevailing road or traffic conditions.
- Breaking the speed limit.
- Driving at an unsafe speed for the weather conditions.

MAKING PROGRESS

If the learner has never been taught how to make normal progress (phase 1), you should give a full instructional briefing, highlighting the following key points:

- Making progress to suit varying road and traffic conditions.
- Avoidance of undue hesitancy.

It is highly important that you draw the learner's attention to the fact that he is travelling too slowly or taking too long to move off. This is particularly important at traffic lights if the learner is staring into space and not paying attention. Stress that effort must be made to use the accelerator to build up the speed of the car, changing up through the gears where necessary. He must endeavour to keep up with the flow of traffic, within the speed limit. Encourage the learner to anticipate the opposite lights changing. There is no harm in moving into first gear providing it is safe and the parking brake is not released for obvious safety reasons, before the lights change. The learner must be aware of the need to keep the car moving at give way junctions if it is safe to do so. He must not be overcautious to the point of becoming a nuisance. Tell the learner that if he stalls the engine he can restart in first gear, with the clutch pedal down on level ground.

Explain that a high percentage of driving test candidates fail for undue hesitancy or not driving at realistic speeds for the conditions because they desperately try to please the examiner by attempting to show how careful they are. This is the wrong approach. If the learner is allowed to continually drive slowly, other drivers may get frustrated or aggressive and may take silly risks to get in front. You must ensure that the learner is made fully aware of the dangers of driving slowly. Finally, don't allow other drivers to get you or the learner upset if they use their horn. You should remain calm and collected, and the learner will not panic or get frustrated (see figure 32).

Figure 32. Making progress.

SOME COMMON FAULTS COMMITTED BY LEARNERS: MAKING PROGRESS

- Not driving at a speed appropriate to the road and traffic conditions.
- Not moving off at road junctions when a safe gap appears.
- Staying in a low gear too long.
- Reducing speed too early whilst approaching a road junction.
- Not maintaining the correct speed whilst driving.
- Taking too long preparing to move off at road junctions or during any of the manoeuvring exercises.

GENERAL ROAD POSITIONING

It is difficult to give a practical demonstration to a learner with regard to general road positioning. If the learner has never been taught how to position the car correctly on the road (phase 1), you should give a full instructional briefing, highlighting the following key points.

- Not hugging the middle of the road or driving in the gutter.
- Driving in the centre of the correct lane.
- Obey the keep left rule except under special circumstances.
- Early observation of road signs and markings.

Explain to the learner that the first rule of the road is to keep to the left. In normal driving the correct position from the kerb is approximately 90 cm (3 feet). If he gets any closer than that there is either a danger of picking up debris from the gutter or even striking the kerb. The learner may have to give up the "keep to the left" position if there is a possibility of danger ahead. For example, if children are fooling around at the side of the road it would be far safer to move into the outside lane.

Explain to the learner that if he is approaching traffic lights, crossroads or roundabouts and intends to proceed straight ahead, he would normally keep to the left unless road markings direct otherwise. If the learner is turning right from a main road into a side road, he should position the car just to the left of centre of the road, unless turning right out of a narrow road, in which case keep well left.

Make sure the learner understands the dangers of hogging the middle of the road (policing the road) or driving too near the kerb especially when pedestrians are in the vicinity. Encourage the learner to look well ahead and to plan his driving so that he will be able to move into the best safety line position, should the road situation ahead change. Point out the advantages of reading road signs and obeying road markings in good time. Stress the dangers of changing lanes unnecessarily or suddenly without using the Mirrors (Look, Assess, Decide), Signal, Manoeuvre routine (see figure 33).

Encourage the learner to always drive in the middle of the lane unless there is a legitimate reason for changing lane and point out the dangers of straddling lane markings. Finally, encourage the learner to use a systematic scanning method, *Look well ahead - check warning signs - look well ahead - check the mirrors to observe the position and actions of other drivers - look well ahead* (see figure 34).

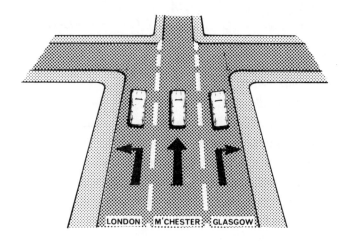

Figure 33. Sometimes you will have to obey road markings in order to reach your destination.

Figure 34. General road positioning.

SOME COMMON FAULTS COMMITTED BY LEARNERS: POSITIONING AND PASSING STATIONARY VEHICLES

- Not keeping left during normal driving.
- Driving too far from the kerb.
- Straddling lanes when it is unsafe.
- Hogging the middle of the road.
- Driving with the wheels in the gutter or too near to the kerb.
- Changing lanes unnecessarily.
- Weaving in and out between parked vehicles.
- Not returning to the left after overtaking when it was safe.
- Failing to position the car correctly when dealing with traffic lights, pedestrian crossings, roundabouts, one way streets and dual carriageways.
- Failing to keep a safe distance from the vehicle in front.
- Driving too close to parked vehicles.
- Allowing insufficient clearance when passing cyclists and animals.

Lesson 13 - Overtaking, meeting and crossing the path of other vehicles

If the learner has never been taught how to overtake other vehicles and cyclists (phase 1), you should give a full instructional briefing, highlighting the following key points:

- The Mirrors (Look, Assess, Decide), Signal, Manoeuvre routine.
- Overtake other vehicles and cyclists safely.
- Follow behind other vehicles at a safe distance.
- Anticipate the actions of pedestrians, cyclists and other drivers.
- Allow adequate clearance to stationary vehicles.

Before overtaking any vehicle the learner must ask himself:

- Would I be breaking the law if I overtake?
- Can I overtake safely?
- Does my car have enough speed and power to overtake?
- Can I safely get back into my own lane on time?
- Do I have a safe gap to move back in?
- Is it necessary?

Remember the golden rule, *If in doubt : DON'T.* Provide practice in situations where overtaking may be carried out safely. Many learners try to acquire their driving licence as quickly as possible. You should never encourage a learner to sit the driving test until you are completely satisfied that he can overtake safely (see figure 35).

Explain that overtaking is one of the most dangerous and hazardous manoeuvres for any driver to execute because it involves crossing onto the other side of the road with the obvious risks caused by oncoming traffic. Emphasise that overtaking can be a safe manoeuvre if properly executed. It is important that you encourage the learner to make progress and to overtake safely where progress is severely held up by slow moving vehicles. You must explain in simple detail why the Mirrors (Look, Assess, Decide), Signal, Manoeuvre, Position, Speed and Look routine are reversed (see figure 36).

Figure 35. If in doubt, don't overtake.

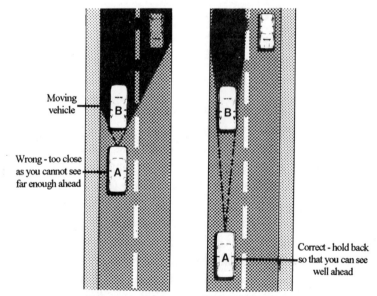

Moving vehicle

Wrong - too close as you cannot see far enough ahead

Correct - hold back so that you can see well ahead

Figure 36. Overtaking a moving vehicle.

OVERTAKING A MOVING VEHICLE

Explain to the learner that when he approaches the rear of the slower moving vehicle he must keep a safe distance behind it. Before overtaking, the learner should use the Position, Speed, Look, Mirrors (Look, Assess, Decide), Signal, Manoeuvre routine. The learner must first **POSITION - HOLDBACK,** no less than two seconds back from the vehicle ahead, keeping out so that he can see past the vehicle in front. If travelling at the same speed as the moving vehicle, he may have to drop a gear(s) to match his speed. The learner must also have the correct acceleration to get past the vehicle in front. He must be aware of the acceleration capability of the car so that he can move out of the "danger period" as soon as possible.

The learner should look well ahead for oncoming traffic, junctions or hazards before deciding to overtake. If it is completely safe ahead, behind, and to the sides of the car he should overtake the vehicle with determination, holding the steering wheel firmly and allowing plenty of clearance. Remember, the learner will be on the wrong side of the road, and the less time spent there, the better.

Instruct the learner to hold a parallel course until the vehicle overtaken is visible in the interior mirror. By doing this, he will have moved back in, well ahead of the overtaken vehicle, and will not have caused it to slow down or change direction. This will also allow space for another overtaking vehicle to pull in. There is no need to signal the intention to move back in because other drivers will expect him to drive on the left-hand side of the road. Explain about the need to be able to see well ahead to look out for 'dead' ground.

Make sure that the learner gauges the length of the vehicle he wishes to overtake. If the vehicle being overtaken is a Large Goods Vehicle he should hold well back to give the best possible view past the lorry so that he can overtake once he can see that there are no hazards ahead. The learner must be very careful because large vehicles can often obscure hazards. If he gauges the length of the vehicle correctly he will be able to judge how much further he will have to travel before pulling back onto his own side of the road safely.

Point out to the learner that he should never overtake unless he has considered how quickly the combined speed will close the gap in which he has chosen to overtake. For example, if travelling at 40 mph and a vehicle approaching in the distance is travelling at 40 mph, this makes a total approach speed of 80 mph.

The learner must be reassured that the "Don't Know" situation is perfectly normal, and not a sign of weakness or uncertainty. Reassure the learner that this decision is the sign of a responsible, patient and confident driver and it will show that he is planning his driving by holding back until he receives more information and then making the correct driving decision.

SOME COMMON FAULTS COMMITTED BY LEARNERS: OVERTAKING

- Not making effective use of the mirrors before and after overtaking.
- Overtaking at an unsafe or illegal place.
- Breaking the speed limit.
- Not holding far enough back from the vehicle or cyclist before overtaking.
- Cutting back in too quickly or too early after overtaking.
- Not allowing a safe clearance when overtaking a moving vehicle.
- Not allowing sufficient clearance to cyclists.
- Not selecting the correct gear prior to overtaking.
- Forcing other traffic from the opposite direction to swerve or slow
- Failing to overtake with determination.
- Failing to hold a parallel course when overtaking.
- Failing to anticipate the actions of other road users.
- Signalling unnecessarily before overtaking.
- Failing to be decisive.

MEETING OTHER VEHICLES SAFELY

If the learner has never been taught how to meet other vehicles safely (phase 1), you should give a full instructional briefing, highlighting the following key points:

- The Mirrors (Look, Assess, Decide) Signal, Manoeuvre routine.
- Approach at a safe speed and provide adequate clearance when meeting traffic coming from the opposite direction.

Take the learner to areas where he will come across this driving situation. Encourage the learner to hold well back from the obstruction and stress the importance of good forward planning and steering a steady course past the obstruction. Encouraging the learner to look well ahead will enable him to make clear and effective driving decisions. Make the learner aware of the dangers involved when meeting other vehicles and stress that such situations are caused by poor anticipation (see figure 37).

Figure 37. Do not be the meat in the sandwich!

Use a visual aid to explain to the learner that in narrow roads a situation may arise where another vehicle is approaching from the opposite direction and there is only one parked vehicle (or obstruction) on the other side of the road, yet it is still causing a constriction of traffic. On this occasion he will normally have priority, unless the other vehicle has already started to move out. Explain that although the learner may have priority under certain circumstances, it is courteous and prudent to give way, for example to large vehicles travelling uphill.

Some learners make the mistake of watching the other driver so intently that they think their car has stopped, when it is actually still moving. On this occasion the learner eventually gets too close to the stationary obstruction and ends up having to reverse. This situation should never occur if the learner understands the principles involved in giving way to oncoming traffic. Explain to the learner that he must, *"Never be the meat in the sandwich"*. In other words he must never get caught in between two vehicles as anything may happen and he could be trapped with no place to go. Stress that a good drive always looks well ahead, scans the area for any possible signs of danger and acts as the situation demands.

SOME COMMON FAULTS COMMITTED BY LEARNERS: MEETING OTHER VEHICLES

- Poor forward observations leading to late and hurried driving decisions.
- Failing to be decisive.
- Failing to provide adequate clearance to approaching traffic.
- Failing to anticipate the actions of other road users.
- Not using the Mirrors (Look, Assess, Decide), Signal, Manoeuvre routine.
- Meeting other vehicles too fast.
- Not giving way to oncoming traffic when they have right of way.

CROSSING THE PATH OF OTHER VEHICLES SAFELY

If the learner has never been taught how to cross the path of other vehicles safely (phase 1), you should give a full instructional briefing, highlighting the following key points:

- Give way to traffic closely approaching from the opposite direction.
- Before turning right, anticipate the actions of pedestrians and give way to them if they are crossing or attempting to cross the road.

Explain to the learner that when turning right from a main road into a side road he may sometimes have to give way to oncoming vehicles. However, he must judge the speed of the approaching vehicle and decide whether if it is safe to turn in front of it. If he is in any doubt, he must wait until the oncoming vehicle has passed. Explain to the learner that rushing into a right turn, to beat an oncoming vehicle can be a foolish and dangerous practice.

The best way to judge if it is safe to turn is to ask, *"Is there any possibility that I may make the oncoming vehicle slow down or alter its course?"* If the answer is "yes", then the learner must wait. On the other hand if the answer is "no", then he may turn in front of the other vehicle. However, he cannot turn if there is a pedestrian either crossing or about to cross the road into which he is turning. Stress to the learner that he must always be prepared to give way. Encourage the learner to make a final right-hand mirror check before actually decides to turn, in case someone is foolish enough to overtake at the junction.

Giving a practical demonstration to the learner would not be feasible on this subject. You should allow him to practice crossing the path of other vehicles until you are sure that he can do it safely and both judgement and timing are perfect. The learner will need much more time than an experienced driver as judgement will be poor and he will be indecisive. It is therefore your responsibility to say when it is safe to cross the path of other vehicles safely (see figure 38).

A useful exercise is to sit at the side of the road and observe approaching vehicles. The learner should imagine that he wishes to turn right and should look for appropriate gaps in the traffic. The instructor may then ask the learner at which point he would choose to make the turn - i.e. which "gaps" would be safe. This builds up the learner's judgement skills before having to undergo the much more practical situation of turning right through fast moving traffic. It is highly important that the learner builds up his own judgement as to whether it is safe to cross the path of other vehicles. Furthermore, it is crucial that you develop the learner's awareness of the very real risks associated with crossing the path of other vehicles.

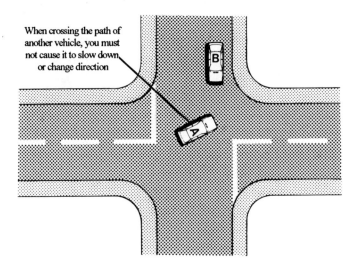

When crossing the path of another vehicle, you must not cause it to slow down, or change direction

Figure 38. Crossing the path of another vehicle.

SOME COMMON FAULTS COMMITTED BY LEARNERS: CROSSING THE PATH OF OTHER VEHICLES

- Failing to give priority to oncoming traffic when making a right turn.
- Cutting in front of closely approaching traffic.
- Making other vehicles stop, reduce speed or swerve.
- Not looking for danger into the side road before turning.
- Failing to give way to pedestrians whilst crossing the path of other vehicles. Being indecisive.

Chapter 6

Lesson 14 - Dealing with traffic lights and pedestrian crossings

Explain to the learner that traffic lights are a set of coloured lights normally found at road junctions and they are used to control the flow of traffic. It is important that he observes traffic lights early and treats them with caution. Explain the correct procedure to be adopted when approaching traffic lights and the sequence of traffic light signals:

- RED means "STOP", wait behind the stop line on the carriageway.
- RED and AMBER also mean "STOP". Do not pass through or start until GREEN shows.
- GREEN means go only if the way is clear. He must take special care if turning left or right and give way to pedestrians who are crossing.
- AMBER means "STOP" at the stop line. He may go on only if the AMBER appears after he has crossed the stop line or is so close to it that to pull up might cause an accident.

Encourage the learner to use the Mirrors (Look, Assess, Decide), Signal, Manoeuvre routine in good time. If he checks the mirrors in good time, he will be able to decide if it is safe to stop should the traffic lights change from green to amber. Encourage the learner to check traffic lights and approach at speeds which permit him to stop if required.

Make sure the learner understands the rules and the very real risks associated with traffic lights. Ensure that the learner does not make superficial head movements and encourage him to look into side roads for any signs of possible danger. Ask the learner what he can actually see to ensure he is taking effective observation. When the learner approaches traffic lights he must know **where** to look, **what** to look out for, **what** to expect and **where** to stop (see figure 39).

Explain to the learner that he must be prepared to give way to pedestrians who may be crossing at the lights even if they are depicting green. Turning right at traffic lights is one of the most hazardous manoeuvres for the learner. You should therefore be particularly careful and observant during this exercise.

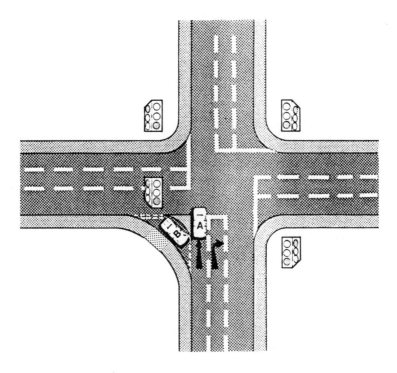

Figure 39. Be prepared to stop at give way lines if it is not safe to proceed.

SOME COMMON FAULTS COMMITTED BY LEARNERS: TRAFFIC LIGHTS

- Not using the Mirrors (Look, Assess, Decide), Signal, Manoeuvre routine.
- Not taking effective observations when emerging through a green light.
- Not observing or complying with a filter light.
- Not anticipating the actions of oncoming traffic when turning right.
- Failing to comply with a red traffic light.
- Approaching traffic lights too fast.
- Failing to recognise that the traffic lights have changed to green.
- Not taking the correct action when the traffic lights change from green to amber.

DEALING WITH PEDESTRIAN CROSSINGS

If the learner has never been taught how to deal with pedestrian crossings (phase 1), give a full instructional briefing, highlighting the following key points:

- Use the Mirrors (Look, Assess, Decide), Signal, Manoeuvre routine.
- Approach the crossing at the proper speed.
- Stop at pedestrian crossings when necessary.
- Don't overtake at or on the approach to pedestrian crossings.
- Do not beckon pedestrians to cross.
- Give way to pedestrians when turning.
- Give proper, well-timed arm signals.
- Explain to the learner the four different types of crossing; pelican, zebra, puffin and toucan.
- Use diagrams so that the learner will understand what your are describing.
- Judge correctly between necessary and unnecessary signals.

When you are explaining the various types of pedestrian crossing keep your explanation as short and as simple as possible. Deal with one type of crossing at a time or you will totally confuse the learner. Explain that when driving in a busy area, he is likely to come across a pedestrian crossing. Emphasise that pedestrians have certain rights of way at pedestrian crossings.

The learner should always be looking well ahead and be prepared to slow down or stop to give way to pedestrians if there is any possibility that a pedestrian could step onto the crossing. It is of paramount importance that he shows caution because the pedestrian may be blind, deaf or handicapped. The learner must regulate speed correctly on the approach to the crossing. If he does not, he may have to give way to a pedestrian at the last moment with the car screeching to a halt. This may result in another vehicle crashing into the rear of the car.

On the approach to a pedestrian crossing the learner should apply the Mirrors (Look, Assess, Decide), Signal, Manoeuvre routine. If he cannot see the kerb properly because of parked vehicles or some other type of obstruction, he should show caution by selecting a lower gear. This also applies if there are pedestrians near or at the crossing. A lower gear is selected because it gives the learner more control over the car on the approach to the crossing, and he will be able to accelerate out of any trouble much faster, if he reaches the point of no return.

Encourage the learner to look well ahead and scan both the pedestrian crossing and the surrounding area for any signs of danger. Point out the dangers that he may come across and what action he should take. Encourage the learner always to have respect for pedestrians who are crossing, even when the traffic lights are at green. Stress the dangers and consequences of beckoning pedestrians to cross, and give reasons why the learner should never overtake whilst approaching the crossing (see figure 40).

Point out the advantages of giving a slowing down arm signal in good time. Allow the learner to wind his window down so that he can practice a slowing down arm signal whilst the car is in motion (but mention that this is discretionary). Highlight the dangers of pedestrian crossings appearing shortly after the learner has emerged from a junction (or turned a corner), as he may be coming from a "blind spot" for the pedestrian. Question the learner to make sure he fully understands the rules governing pedestrian crossings. It is crucial that the learner understands the rules, and the very real risks associated with pedestrian crossings. The learner must know **where** to look, **where** to stop, **what** to look for, and **how** to react to actual and potential danger, when dealing with pedestrian crossings.

Figure 40. Regulate your speed correctly when approaching a pedestrian crossing.

SOME COMMON FAULTS COMMITTED BY LEARNERS: PEDESTRIAN CROSSINGS

- Not using the Mirrors (Look, Assess, Decide), Signal, Manoeuvre routine.
- Approaching the crossing too fast.
- Failing to anticipate the actions of pedestrians.
- Not stopping at the crossing where necessary.
- Not allowing pedestrians sufficient time to finish crossing.
- Beckoning pedestrians to cross.
- Not proceeding at a pelican crossing when the traffic lights turn to flashing amber, if it is not safe to do so.
- Overtaking on the approach to or at the crossing.

Lesson 15 - Dealing with roundabouts

Explain to the learner that a roundabout is a road junction at which traffic moves one way around a central island. Roundabouts can be many different shapes and sizes but they are designated to help traffic flow by mixing streams of traffic with the minimum amount of delay. Explain to the learner the importance of using the Mirrors (Look, Assess, Decide), Signal, Manoeuvre routine and approaching under control at the proper speed.

Encourage the learner to start looking to the right early before making any commitment to proceed. It is highly important that you brief the learner very carefully before driving on the roundabout. If the learner is not briefed properly, he may lose his sense of direction on the roundabout, "bluffing" you by taking the correct exit simply by chance and you will be none the wiser. Question the learner to make sure he fully understands the rules governing roundabouts.

Use visual aids to emphasise to the learner that he should give way to traffic from the immediate right and stop where necessary. When the learner approaches a roundabout he must know **where** to look, **what** to look out for, and **what** to expect. Initially, talk the learner through this exercise, from every direction, stage-by-stage, until he can do it competently. Later, allow him to practice without any talk through. You will be surprised how difficult it is for learners to grasp roundabouts correctly. With plenty of patience, practice and headache tablets, you will succeed.

Stress the dangers and consequences of suddenly changing direction on a roundabout without first checking the mirrors. The learner must understand that larger vehicles require more berth especially Large Goods Vehicles drawing trailers. They may have to manoeuvre into an unusual position whilst negotiating a roundabout (see figure 41). Using the 'clock method', show the learner how he should deal with a roundabout depending on which direction he wishes to travel.

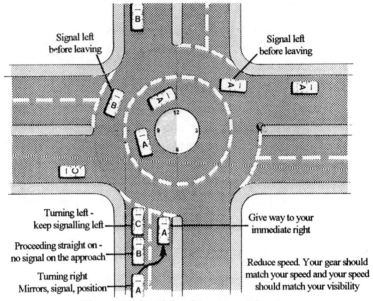

Figure 41. Dealing with a roundabout.

SOME COMMON FAULTS COMMITTED BY LEARNERS: ROUNDABOUTS

- Not using the Mirrors (Look, Assess, Decide), Signal, Manoeuvre routine.
- Not giving way to traffic from the immediate right.
- Not emerging onto the roundabout when a suitable gap appears.
- Approaching the roundabout too fast.
- Not looking early enough to monitor traffic whilst approaching the roundabout.
- Not positioning the car correctly before or during negotiating the roundabout.
- Changing lanes unnecessarily when negotiating the roundabout.
- Not leaving the roundabout by the clearest, most convenient exit.
- Signalling too early or too late when approaching or leaving the roundabout.
- Negotiating the roundabout in the wrong gear.
- Failing to anticipate the actions of other road users.

Lesson 16 - Dealing with box junctions and dual carriageways

DEALING WITH BOX JUNCTIONS

Explain to the learner that some road junctions, particularly busy junctions controlled by traffic lights are called box junctions. At box junctions, criss-cross yellow lines cover the centre of the junction and are designed to permit the free flow of cross traffic. It is important that the learner understands the rules governing box junctions. Explain to the learner that the golden rule at box junctions is never to enter it unless the exit road is clear.

However, there is one exception to this rule. If the learner wants to turn right and the exit road is clear, he may enter the box junction even though the car is obstructed by oncoming traffic. In this situation, he should position the car and wait in the area marked with yellow lines until there is a safe gap to complete the turn. If there is another vehicle in front waiting to turn right, he may wait behind this vehicle. The learner must be careful because another vehicle coming towards him may want to turn right as well and he must not obstruct it from doing so.

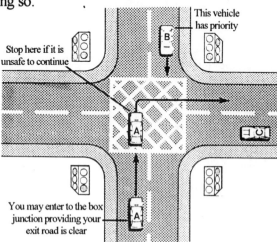

Figure 42. Dealing with box junctions.

Question the learner to make sure he fully understands the rules associated with box junctions. Give the learner plenty of practice turning right at box junctions. Tell the learner **where** to look, **what** to look out for, and to **how** to anticipate the actions of oncoming traffic (see figure 42).

DEALING WITH DUAL CARRIAGEWAYS
Explain to the learner that a dual carriageway is a two-lane road (or more), normally divided by a central reservation, where traffic travels in different directions on either side of the reservation (see figure 43).

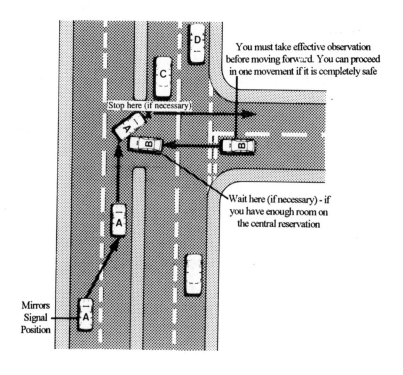

Figure 43. Dealing with dual carriageways.

Point out that he must not become overwhelmed with so much fast moving traffic and visual stimulation going on around (information overload). He therefore ends up missing things that he should be observing. The information overload situation can be avoided if he looks well ahead, scans the area and is selective in what he sees. You should permit the learner to drive on different types of dual carriageways and encourage him to drive at the maximum speed possible (conditions permitting). This will boost confidence and is essential for future driving after he has passed the driving test.

Encourage the learner to look well ahead to avoid late and hurried driving decisions, and apply the Mirrors (Look, Assess, Decide), Signal, Manoeuvre routine as early as possible. Point out the consequences and dangers of failing to do this. Remind the learner that traffic may move very quickly on dual carriageways and that it is crucial to use the mirrors correctly, to judge the speeds and actions of other vehicles. Also remind the learner to be prepared to give way to other traffic especially when turning right off a dual carriageway. Draw diagrams or show pictures in order to get your message across. Finally question the learner to make sure he fully understands the rules governing dual carriageways.

Chapter 7

Lesson 17 - The emergency stop

If the learner has never been taught how to carry out an emergency stop (phase 1), you should give a full instructional briefing, highlighting the following key points:

- The importance of quick reactions.
- Application of the footbrake before the clutch.
- Avoidance and correction of skids.
- Keeping both hands on the steering wheel.

Before attempting the emergency stop you must select a safe place to practice this exercise. Permit the learner to practice the exercise whilst stationary (pivot from the accelerator to the footbrake), as this will help him to understand the principles of the emergency stop. Make sure it is safe behind you before you give the signal to stop. After you have finally finished the emergency stop always let the learner know that you will not ask him to do the emergency stop again. If you do not, you may fidget or move your hand and the learner may anticipate another emergency stop resulting in a traffic accident.

Explain to the learner that there are three different types of skids that may occur when driving a motor car: a front-wheel skid, a rear-wheel skid and a four-wheel skid. There are also four main causes of skidding: excessive speed, harsh braking, fierce acceleration and erratic steering. Also explain that a good driver never gets caught in a skid. If he is looking well ahead and driving at a speed appropriate to the road and traffic conditions, a skid should never happen.

Give a practical demonstration to the learner and show how much brake to apply, stressing the importance of firm but progressive braking. Explain how to avoid skids and which way to turn the steering wheel should the wheels lock. You could use a toy car or something similar to demonstrate skidding. Remember the saying, *"What I see, I remember."* (See figure 44).

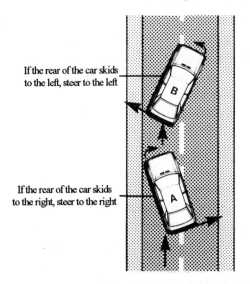

If the rear of the car skids to the left, steer to the left

If the rear of the car skids to the right, steer to the right

Figure 44. Controlling a skid.

There will be a tendency for the learner to worry about the emergency stop after it has been completed which may lead to a lack of concentration or possible careless driving. Tell the learner to get the emergency stop right out his mind as soon as it is over. Highlight the dangers of not checking the mirrors and looking all round before moving off. If the learner queries the use of mirrors before conducting an emergency stop, point out the dangers in this and emphasise the importance of using the mirrors frequently in case an emergency does happen.

SOME COMMON FAULTS COMMITTED BY LEARNERS: EMERGENCY STOP

- Checking the mirror before stopping.
- Not stopping quickly enough.
- Not reacting quickly enough.
- Not braking firmly and progressively.
- Not reacting when given the command to stop.
- Slow reaction when given the command to stop.
- Locking the wheels causing the car to skid.
- Turning the steering wheel the wrong way when the car skids.
- Applying or reaching for the parking brake before stopping.
- Removing one hand from the steering wheel before stopping.
- Applying the clutch before the footbrake.
- Applying the footbrake and the clutch at the same time.
- Not observing properly after the emergency stop.
- Moving off when unsafe to do so after the emergency stop.
- Not applying the parking brake or selecting neutral after stopping.
- Failing to release the parking brake before moving off.

Lesson 18 - The driving test, the Highway Code and some myths

THE DRIVING TEST - FOOD FOR THOUGHT
Most learners fail their driving test because of insufficient instruction and practice. A good driving instructor has the knowledge and experience to judge when a learner driver is ready to sit the driving test. **Never** allow a learner to sit the driving test too soon. He should learn how to **drive** - not how to pass the driving test. He will be ready to sit the test as soon as he can drive and manoeuvre the car consistently and with confidence without supervision or guidance from the instructor, gained plenty of experience with different types of road and traffic conditions, and developed good road sense.

THE DAY OF THE TEST
You must ensure that the learner arrives at the test centre early, allowing sufficient time to park the car close to the centre. He should park in a legal, safe and convenient place. Make sure his car displays "L" plates at the front and rear of his car - avoid putting them on the windows. The car he uses must be properly licensed, registered and insured. The seat belts must be clean, untangled and they must work properly. It is important that all the windows, lights and indicators are clean and he should remove all stickers and mascots (e.g. fluffy dice) that may impair vision. The learner should sit in the waiting room at least ten minutes before the scheduled time of the test. Tell the learner not to worry about anyone else talking because you've heard more rubbish coming from the test centre waiting room than a psychiatrist's treatment surgery. Make sure the learner has his provisional driving licence (check it is signed) and appointment card.

ENTER THE EXAMINER
When the driving examiner calls the candidate's name, the learner should greet him with a smile to show him that he is confident. The examiner will ask him to sign his name on a driving test report form,

and then request that he leads the way to the vehicle. If he does not understand English very well, or he is deaf and unable to speak, he may take an interpreter but the learner must ask the examiner for permission. The interpreter must not be the driving instructor and must not interfere with the conduct of the test in any way.

Sometimes two examiners will be present at the test. The Supervising Examiner is testing the first examiner and will sit in the back seat to ensure the examiner is testing the learner within the Driving Standard Agency's guidelines. The Supervising Examiner will not interfere with the conduct of the test, and does not have the authority to overrule the examiner's decision.

THE EYESIGHT TEST

The examiner will then ask the learner to read a number plate of a stationary vehicle over the prescribed distance. If unsuccessful, he will bring him closer to the vehicle and give him another chance. Should the learner fail this test, the examiner will use a measuring tape to determine the precise distance. If unsuccessful on this occasion, the candidate fails the test. Once the learner has passed the eyesight test, the examiner will ask him to get into his vehicle and make himself comfortable.

When the examiner has checked the learner's car he will then say, *"Follow the road ahead unless the traffic signs or road markings direct you otherwise, or unless I ask you to turn, which I'll do in good time. Move off when you are ready please."* The examiner will not normally use the words corner, crossroads, junctions or traffic lights. It is the learner's responsibility to recognise that they are coming up and he must deal with them accordingly.

SAFETY CHECKS BEFORE STARTING THE ENGINE

When the learner gets into the vehicle he should check the following:

- The parking brake is on.
- All the doors are properly closed.

- Adjust the seat (if necessary).
- Fasten the seatbelt.
- Make sure the mirrors are properly adjusted.
- That the gear is in the neutral position.

Tell the learner not to waste time by taking a long time over these checks. The seat and the mirrors should already be in the correct position if he drove the car to the test centre. The learner must start the engine and carry out the Preparation, Observation and Move routine before moving off.

TIPS FOR THE TEST
Explain to the learner that during the test, he must make sure that he uses the accelerator, clutch, gears, footbrake, parking brake and steering properly and smoothly. He must move away safely and under control. The learner must always depress the clutch just before stopping. If he stalls the engine, he should remain calm and simply apply the parking brake and select neutral. Inform the learner to use the correct gear for the speed and the road conditions, and to change gear at the correct time before any hazard or bends on the road. Inform the learner to never coast by letting the car run with the gear lever in neutral.

He should neither look at the examiner nor down at the foot and hand controls whilst driving. The learner should avoid late or harsh braking. In most situations, only firm pressure is needed to brake safely. He must avoid overuse of the parking brake, but apply it where necessary. The examiner will expect him to drive with the traditional "push and pull" method whilst turning and not to steer too early or too late. The learner must steer in a controlled and safe manner. Make sure he carries out the Mirrors (Look, Assess, Decide), Signal, Manoeuvre routine before making any driving decision.

MOVING AWAY

Explain to the learner that the examiner will expect him to move off safely and under control on level ground, from behind a parked vehicle and on uphill and downhill gradients. Make sure he releases the parking brake and always check his Mirrors, Look, Assess, Decide and give a signal if any road users would benefit. The learner must remember to check the blind spot by looking round for traffic and pedestrians. He must never move off if to do so would make another vehicle or cyclist slow down or alter course. The learner must follow the road ahead unless the examiner dictates otherwise. The examiner will give directions in good time, in a clear and unmistakable manner. The examiner will not try to trick him because he is there to ensure that the learner is a safe and competent driver and he will not expect him to drive perfectly. The examiner will be polite and respectful and the learner will drive on routes specially selected for the driving test which will include all types of roads and traffic conditions.

MAKING NORMAL PROGRESS

Tell the learner to drive normally, make normal progress and try to keep up with the flow of traffic - conditions permitting. He must build up speed before changing into a higher gear and avoid selecting first gear for every turn. He will probably come across some give way junctions or crossroads. Make sure he regulates his speed on the approach. He must drive straight ahead unless told otherwise. The learner must not take too long to prepare for moving off, and avoid hanging around junctions waiting for something to happen. Many learners desperately try to please the examiner by being overcautious but they usually end up becoming a nuisance, and fail their test for undue hesitancy.

THE EMERGENCY STOP

Explain to the learner that as soon as his examiner gives the signal to stop, he must stop as soon as possible and under full control. Once he has completed the emergency stop, the examiner will say, *"Thank you. I shall not ask you to carry out that exercise again. Drive on when you are ready, please"*. This avoids him thinking that another emergency stop instruction has been given if the examiner fidgets or makes any movement with his hand. Make sure that he checks over both shoulders before moving off again. If a real emergency stop arises during the test, there may be no need to conduct this exercise.

MANOEUVRING EXERCISES
Explain to the learner that soon after he has moved off, the examiner may ask him to stop and reverse the car into a side road and park behind a stationary vehicle. He may then be asked to turn the car round in the road, using forward to reverse gears so that it is facing the opposite direction. The learner should always proceed under low-speed control making proper use of the clutch, accelerator, brakes and steering to achieve reasonable accuracy. The learner should avoid striking the kerb and must keep a look out, giving way to other vehicles and pedestrians during the manoeuvring exercises.

CARE IN THE USE OF SPEED
Inform the learner that once he has completed all his manoeuvres, he should be prepared to deal with any hazards he may come across. The learner must watch that the speed does not break the speed limit and he must not drive too fast for the road and traffic conditions. Ensure that he can stop safely in the distance he can see to be clear. The learner should always keep a safe distance from the vehicle in front. He must remember that if the vehicle is travelling at 30 mph, it will cover approximately 14 metres (45 feet) every second. There's an old saying, *"When skating over thin ice, be wise with speed"*.

GENERAL ROAD POSITIONING
Explain to the learner to keep to the left during normal driving unless there is a legitimate reason for not doing so. When approaching roundabouts, make sure that he takes the correct lane on the approach to and throughout the roundabout. Where lanes are marked,

he should keep to the middle of the lane if possible; the learner must not hug the middle of the road or drive in the gutter. It is important that he keeps looking well ahead to avoid weaving in and out between parked vehicles. Remind the learner that if he has to overtake another vehicle, he must always move back into the left-hand side of the road, conditions permitting, as soon as he can see the vehicle overtaken appear in the interior mirror.

DEALING WITH ROAD JUNCTIONS

Explain to the learner that he must keep a good look out for give way junctions and any unmarked crossroads and be prepared to stop if necessary. If he does stop, he should avoid allowing the car to cross the markings painted on the road or past the kerbline of the junction. The learner must regulate speed on the approach and take effective observation before moving into the new road. If turning right, he should position the car just left to the centre of the road. However, he should keep well left if turning right out of a narrow road and avoid cutting the corner. If turning left he should normally keep over to the left and not swing out. The learner must always give way to pedestrians who are crossing the road.

ACTING ON SIGNS AND SIGNALS

Explain the need to act properly if he comes across any **STOP** signs, red traffic lights or markings on the road. He should never proceed through a green traffic light unless the way is clear and must obey all signals given by police officers, traffic wardens and school crossing patrols.

DEALING WITH PEDESTRIAN CROSSINGS

It is important that the learner keeps looking well ahead and if he sees a pedestrian crossing, he must exercise care and be prepared to give a slowing down arm signal if it would help other road users. He should stop at the crossing and drive on only when it is legal and safe.

OVERTAKING, MEETING AND CROSSING THE PATH OF OTHER VEHICLES SAFELY

He should allow enough room when overtaking another vehicle or cyclist and must not cut in too sharply after overtaking. If the road narrows and the learner is in any doubt whether there is enough room for two vehicles, he should hold back and let the approaching vehicle through. Remember, *"Never be the meat in the sandwich".*

ALERTNESS AND ANTICIPATION

Explain to the learner that if the examiner passes any comment about his driving during the test, it does not mean that he has failed. If an examiner takes verbal action, the candidate fails. Examiners are human - they do not fail learners because they do not like their face. If he is good enough as a driver, the examiner will pass him but of course they are approached by many candidates who are clearly not properly prepared for the test. An examiner is a professional and recognises mistakes caused by nerves as opposed to a learner not being properly trained for the test. It is crucial that the learner always looks well ahead and thinks before he makes any driving decision. He should try to anticipate what other road users will do, including pedestrians, and act accordingly.

Figure 45. "Have I passed?"

PASS OR FAIL

The examiner will pass the candidate providing that no serious or dangerous faults have been committed. If the learner passes, the examiner will ask for his licence and to sign the pass certificate. However, if he fails, the examiner will complete a statement of failure form, on which will be marked the points which caused the failure (see figure 45). In this section, listed are the most popular questions asked by learner drivers during my career as a driving instructor.

SOME MYTHS AND POPULAR MISCONCEPTIONS
QUESTIONS

Q. Do examiners have a quota of learners to pass each day?
A. No. If the learner is good enough, the examiner will pass him.

Q. Will I fail if I cross my hands on the steering wheel?
A. If the learner crosses his hands and loses control of the steering wheel, the examiner may fail him so use the "push and pull" method.

Q. Will the examiner fail me immediately and tell me to drive back to the test centre if I commit a serious fault at the start of my test?
A. No. The examiner will carry on until the end of the test. However, if a pattern of dangerous driving is displayed, the examiner will terminate the test in the interests of public safety and fail the candidate.

Q. Will the examiner ask me to turn at a junction at the last moment?
A. The examiner will give the learner instructions in good time, in a clear and unmistakable manner.

Q. Is the examiner trying to trick me if the asks me to take the next road on the right and the entrance is marked "**NO ENTRY**"?
A. The examiner will never try to trick the learner. When asked to turn and the road is marked "**NO ENTRY**" he should take the next available road.

Q. Can I restart the engine in gear if I stall?
A. Yes. With experience the learner will have the confidence to restart the engine in first gear, with the clutch pedal down on level ground.

Q. What happens if my car breaks down during the driving test?
A. The examiner will give the learner a couple of minutes to try and rectify the fault. If unable to do this, the test will be terminated and the examiner will return to the test centre. The test fee will be forfeited and he will have to re-apply for another test.

Q. Am I permitted to cut corners in my driving test?
A. Don't cut corners unless completely safe and absolutely necessary.

Q. Do I have to turn my car round in three distinct movements when carrying out the turn in the road exercise?
A. Not necessarily. The amount of turns the learner takes will be dictated by the width of the road and the length of the car.

Q. Can I change gear and turn at the same time?
A. Yes, providing the steering is set on a curved course. Do not attempt to turn and change gear at the same time.

Q. What would the driving examiner do if a learner drove in a dangerous manner during in the driving test?
A. The driving examiner may abandon the candidate's test in the interest of public safety.

Q. Will I fail my driving test if I change from fourth gear straight into second gear?
A. No. Any gear changing method is correct if executed properly and safely.

Chapter 8

Lesson 19 - Automatic transmission, motorway driving and trams

DRIVING WITH AUTOMATIC TRANSMISSION

In this lesson we will look at the way the learner should drive a car fitted with automatic transmission. It is easier and safer to drive an automatic car than a manual car because the learner's hands are in more contact with the steering wheel, there is less gear changing to worry about, and it is less tiring and frustrating whilst driving in traffic. Learning to drive in an automatic car is very useful for older and disabled people. Since it is easier to drive an automatic car it can be dangerous if the learner becomes too confident.

Explain to the learner that exactly the same standard of driving is required with an automatic car in the driving test. Like a manual car, an automatic car does have gears but an automatic car can change itself to a higher gear as the road speed increases and to a lower gear when it decreases. In other words, the gears are changed for him, depending upon the road speed, car load and the position of the accelerator pedal.

Most automatics are fitted with a selector lever with positions usually marked P-R-N-D-2-1. P (Park) and R (Reverse) are usually safe-guarded by notches, so that they are not selected in error. They can be selected when the driver operates a release catch to clear the notch. If you select position "D" (drive), the automatic transmission changes through the gears, both up and down.

However the learner will, under certain circumstances, have to select D.1 and D.2 by manually moving the selector lever. Let us look at the selector positions in more detail starting with the "P" position.

P. *(Parking)*
This position should be used when parking. It mechanically locks the transmission and it should only be selected when the car is stationary with the engine switched off.

R. *(Reverse)*
This position allows the vehicle to move backwards and should only be selected when the car is stationary otherwise it may cause damage to the car.

N. *(Neutral)*
This position means no gear has been selected and the car cannot be driven forwards or backwards.

D. *(Drive)*
This position allows the vehicle to be driven forward and by simply pressing the accelerator pedal the gears will change up or down automatically depending on the road speed, vehicle load and the position of the accelerator.

D. *2*
Many automatic transmissions have three forward gears. Position D2 may be used instead of "D" (Drive), allowing the learner to lock the automatic transmission in second gear. This is a useful gear for moving off on a slippery road surface or when negotiating a roundabout to stop the car running away from the learner when driving down hill.

D. *1*

This position allows the learner to lock the automatic transmission in the first gear position. It is very useful for driving in slow moving traffic or driving down a very long steep hill, because unnecessary gear changes will not take place and he will keep full control of his car.

THE PARKING/HAND BRAKE

Explain to the learner the purpose of the parking brake is to secure the car for safety reasons when it is stationary or parked. For example, assume that he has stopped the car at a pedestrian crossing, the selector lever is in the D (Drive) position and he accidentally presses the accelerator pedal. If the parking brake is not applied, the car will move forward onto the crossing with potentially dangerous consequences. The learner should also use the parking brake if the car has a tendency to "creep" forward. This may happen if the tick-over of the engine gives enough drive to move the car. Many drivers rely on creep to hold the car on an uphill gradient. However, this could be dangerous as the car may roll back without warning if the engine stops for any reason.

MOTORWAY DRIVING

Once the learner has passed the driving test and gained a full licence, he will be permitted to drive on the motorway without a qualified driver accompanying him. He will be driving at very high speeds for the first time, which is safe if carried out with skill and responsibility.

Explain to the newly qualified driver that a motorway is a main road for fast moving traffic with limited access. During this lesson we will cover many aspects of motorway driving so the inexperienced driver will have the right skills and disciplines that will enable him to become an even better and safer driver. It is imperative that he checks the general condition of the car before driving on the motorway because he will probably be driving at high speeds.

The newly qualified driver should always check that the tyres are in good condition, the tyre depth is within the legal limit, the tyre pressures are set correctly, there is enough fuel, oil and adequate water levels and that all the windows, headlights, indicators and mirrors are clean. If drawing a trailer, he should check and secure the load before commencing the journey. If he feels tired or unwell he must not under any circumstances drive on the motorway. He may fall asleep and possibly kill himself or someone else.

Joining and leaving the motorway
Explain to the newly qualified driver that when he joins the motorway, he will approach from a road called a slip road. As he comes off the slip road he will enter the acceleration lane. The acceleration lane will allow him to adjust his speed so that it matches the speed of the traffic already on the motorway. Make sure he stays in the acceleration lane (and not drive on the hard shoulder) until it is safe to enter the motorway in the first lane.

The newly qualified driver must not force his way onto the motorway. Judging the speed of the motorway traffic before he emerges requires skill and patience, because traffic will be moving very fast. He should stay in the first lane until he has become accustomed to the speeds of other vehicles using the motorway. If he wishes to leave the motorway he will also leave by a slip road. He must keep a good look out for the countdown markers as they will tell him how far away the exit road is. When leaving the motorway he must make sure he adjusts the speed to suit the new conditions. If he misses the exit, he must carry on until he reaches the next exit.

Driving on the motorway
Explain to the newly qualified driver to drive in the first lane unless overtaking or road signs and markings direct otherwise. Some Large Goods Vehicles, coaches or any vehicle drawing a trailer must not use the third lane of a carriageway with three or more lanes unless there are exceptional circumstances. In normal circumstances, the centre

lane is the only one they may use for overtaking. Finally, if he sees a Large Goods Vehicle emerging onto the motorway, it is courteous and prudent to adjust his speed or change lane to allow them access.

The newly qualified driver must watch out for any motorway speed restrictions or flashing light signals which will warn him of any hazards ahead. They will usually seen on overhead gantries or at the side of the carriageway. If he ever sees flashing amber lights, he should check the mirrors and, if it is safe, use progressive braking to slow down (especially in poor weather conditions) until satisfied that it is safe to go faster again. If the car breaks down or something falls off the car, he must move over to the hard shoulder as soon as it is safe. It is highly important that he tries to position the car as far over to the left-hand side of the hard shoulder as possible.

The driver must warn any passengers of the dangers of passing vehicles, and place a warning triangle approximately 150 metres (160 yards) to the rear of the car. This will prevent being struck by another vehicle who may be positioned badly in the first lane. He must look out for a telephone symbol with an arrow to tell him where to find the nearest emergency telephone (these are directly connected to a police control room). He must not under any circumstances cross the central reservation to use an emergency telephone. When rejoining the first lane, he should build up his speed first on the hard shoulder and wait for a safe gap in the traffic before emerging. If he ever feels tired whilst driving on the motorway, he should wind the window down for ventilation and leave the motorway at the next exit or the nearest service station.

Lane discipline

Inform the newly qualified driver that on carriageways with three or more lanes the normal *"Keep to the left"* rule still applies. He may, however, stay in the second lane when there are slower vehicles in the first lane but he should return to the first lane when he has passed them. The third lane is for overtaking only. If he uses it, he should move back to the second lane and then into the first lane as soon as he can without cutting in. It is important that he only overtakes on the left if traffic is moving slowly in queues. Finally, he should always flash his headlights instead of using the horn if he ever wishes to warn other road users of his presence.

Look, assess, decide

After the newly qualified driver has checked his mirrors, he can quickly glance over his shoulder to check for other road users in the blind spot - especially motorcyclists, before deciding to change direction to the right or left. However, if he finds it necessary to check the blind spot, he must be careful because a vehicle in front may make a quick lane change or brake sharply. When driving on the motorway he should always concentrate and look well ahead as far as possible. The earlier he sees any danger, the more time he will have to take evasive action.

Driving at night

When driving on a motorway at night, the newly qualified driver will sometimes see different types of coloured reflective studs. They are a guide to warn and inform. There are amber-coloured studs marking the right-hand edge of the carriageway, red studs between the hard shoulder and carriageway, green studs which separate the acceleration and deceleration lanes from the through carriageway and yellow/bright green studs which are found at contraflow systems and roadworks. If he ever has to overtake another vehicle or obstruction on a motorway at night, he should keep the indicators on longer and signal sooner to warn other traffic.

Motorway fog

When driving in fog, the newly qualified driver must:

- Not hang on to the tail lights of the vehicle in front because it gives a false sense of security. In thick fog, if he can see the vehicle in front he is probably too close unless travelling very slowly.
- See and be seen. If he cannot see clearly use dipped headlights.

- Use front or rear fog lights if visibility is seriously reduced, generally when he cannot see for more than 100 metres (328 feet). Use fog lights at other times and remember to switch them off when visibility improves.
- Use windscreen wipers and demisters.
- Check mirrors and slow down. Keep a safe distance behind the vehicle in front. Always be able to pull up within the distance he can see clearly.
- Be aware of his speed because he may be going much faster than he thinks. He must not accelerate to get away from a vehicle which is too close behind. When slowing down, he must use the brakes so that the brake lights warn drivers behind.
- Be prepared for a bank of fog or drifting smoke ahead when the word `fog' is shown on a roadside signal, but the road appears to be clear. Fog can drift rapidly and is often patchy. Even if it seems to be clearing, he could suddenly find himself back in thick fog. If he must drive in fog, he must allow more time for his journey.

TRAMS

Explain to the learner that trams are being reintroduced into cities throughout the UK to both provide a more efficient public transport system and a more environmentally friendly form of transport. Trams are already prevalent in European cities and have been found to encourage tourism and commerce as a result of their convenience and safety. Other benefits include a fast, frequent and reliable service, relief to road congestion and reduced inner-city parking problems. Tram stops and the vehicles themselves are adapted to cope with the individual needs of the physically handicapped, blind, deaf and those unable to speak. However, with the advent of trams, drivers should take particular note of several points. Here is a check list of do's and don'ts that will both help the learner to keep safe and maintain the smooth running of the tram system:

Do

- Exercise care until he and other drivers are familiar with a different traffic system.
- Treat crossing points the same way as railway crossings.
- Be careful when turning or braking on the steel rails as they may be slippery.
- Obey all signals. Diamond shaped signs give instructions to tram drivers only. When there are no signals, always give way to trams.
- Watch out for trams that run close to the kerb or where the lines move from one side of the road to the other.
- Stop for additional pedestrian crossings where passengers will be embarking and disembarking from the trams.
- Be particularly mindful of cyclists and motorcyclists. Their narrow tyres may put them in danger when they come in contact with the rails.

Don't

- Try to race trams. If he needs to overtake, remember that the trams may be as long as 60 metres (200 feet). Try and overtake at stops if it is safe to do so.
- Drive between platforms at tramway stations. Follow any direction signs.
- Park where the vehicle will obstruct trams or other road users.
- Enter reserved areas for the tramway which are marked either with white line markings or a different type of surface, or both. These are often 'one way', but occasionally 'two way'.
- Be caught out by the speed and silence of the trams.

Lesson 20 - Driving for the physically disabled, the deaf and the unable to speak

VARIOUS ADAPTATIONS

It can be relatively easy for a disabled person to learn to drive providing that the vehicle which is being used has been suitably adapted. If he is unable to drive with standard controls, there are a whole range of adaptations and attachments available which provide both alternative means of controlling the vehicle and for increasing the driver's awareness. Adaptations range from a simple steering ball and cup-to-foot operated steering devices to sophisticated hand-operated accelerator, brake and clutch (right or left hand operation). Such controls are mainly servo or power-assisted to reduce the physical effort involved in their use.

Power-assisted steering is essential where there is muscle weakness around the shoulders and hips. Easier to move selector levers can be fitted if an arm is too weak to work normal gear levers. If a disabled candidate experiences any problems reaching the hand or foot controls, the seat or the foot pedals could be re-positioned to suit the individual. Many people sit on a cushion when they are driving to raise themselves up higher or for added comfort. If the cushion is unsecured, recent tests have shown that this practice may increase the chance of being injured if a traffic accident occurs. Tilting or raising the seat can sometimes overcome any discomfort and place the driver high enough to see clearly over the steering wheel.

Conventional controls can be adapted to overcome certain difficulties, for example, re-positioning the indicator lever or horn. A push button infra-red transmitter can be installed, close to the steering ball, to operate the vehicle's auxiliary controls. Vehicles may be fitted with extra interior and exterior mirrors, for example, bonnet centre-mounted mirrors (for side vision) if the driver cannot turn the head or body. Unmodified automatic transmission will be fully sufficient for persons with left leg amputations or other left leg difficulties.

Automatic cars are the normal choice of car for most disabled people because they greatly diminish the task demands made upon the driver. Furthermore, vehicles fitted with automatic transmission can be easily adapted to overcome a right leg disability by simply moving the accelerator pedal to the left-hand side of the footbrake, allowing the left foot to operate the footbrake and the accelerator. Recent technological developments include remote-controlled steering which enables a severely disabled person to drive safely without the use of any arms.

ENTERING AND EXITING FROM A VEHICLE
Special consideration should be given to how easy it will be for the disabled driver to enter or exit from the vehicle without too much difficulty. Door and seating dimensions are particularly important for the physically handicapped. There are numerous accessories available to help a disabled driver overcome the problem of getting in and out of a vehicle. For example, the disabled driver could have special handles installed by the door pillar or above the driver's door to provide a good firm grip.

THE DRIVING TEST
When a disabled candidate applies for a driving test appointment it is important that any disability is declared on the application form. During a disabled candidates driving test, the examiner will be sympathetic but nevertheless the same standard of competence will be required to pass as with any able-bodied test candidate. The Department of Transport tries to accommodate disabled drivers by making special arrangements for their driving tests. This includes giving priority over non-disabled candidates, allowing extra time to compensate for any difficulty encountered in entering the vehicle and explaining any adaptations of the controls to the examiner. During the test the disabled driver will be exempt from wearing a seatbelt if in possession of a valid medical exemption certificate from a doctor.

However, wearing a seatbelt makes good sense, and will reduce his chance of being seriously injured or killed if involved in a road traffic accident. There are clip-on attachments readily available which make it easier to reach for the seatbelt. If the belt irritates or feels uncomfortable, there are various types of accessories which can be fitted to overcome this problem. It is important to remember that if a disabled person passes the driving test in an adapted vehicle, then the examiner would stipulate that the driver may only drive a vehicle with those adaptations which were used during the test.

DRIVING FOR THE DEAF AND THE UNABLE TO SPEAK

This section aims to teach the basic skills to any professional driving instructor who feels they have the necessary qualities required to teach deaf people to drive correctly and safely on the road. Teaching a learner driver who is deaf and unable to speak requires a great deal of skill. The instructor must be extremely understanding and fully aware of the many problems a deaf person will encounter whilst learning to drive. However, it is important to remember that when a deaf candidate sits the driving test, the same standard of driving is required by a deaf person as with any other test candidate.

The driving test will last approximately one hour, depending on the seriousness of the candidate's disability. This will allow the examiner sufficient time to communicate and relay all the necessary commands to the learner. Before the candidate's test commences the driving examiner should be informed by the instructor of the most effective method of communication which has been used between the learner and the instructor during the pupil's tuition. The examiner will most probably use flash cards and route cards.

GETTING STARTED

If someone is profoundly deaf, hard of hearing or cannot speak, learning to drive should present no real problems, providing that he or she is taught by an understanding, sympathetic and competent professional instructor. Prior to commencing with any driving tuition it is **crucial** to remember that an effective and consistent method of communication must be agreed between the learner and the instructor. This will enable the learner to carry out all the necessary instructions and commands in good time without becoming confused.

Poor communication may result in the learner interpreting you incorrectly with potentially dangerous consequences. The instructor must remember to be constantly vigilant at all times when the learner is driving. This is extremely important because the learner will be unable to hear either other traffic, emergency vehicles or any other danger. The learner must compensate for his or her lack of hearing by a greatly improved perception of what's happening on the road ahead and by observing everything much more closely.

INSTRUCTIONS AND DIRECTIONS ON THE MOVE

An effective method of communication which could be used between the instructor and the learner whilst the car is moving, involves hand and finger signals. An excellent example for the instructor to use could be as follows. Lean forward to attract the learner's attention, then extend the arm out fully to eye level and point with one finger for directing the learner to turn at the first road on the right or left and point with two fingers if you wish the learner to turn at the second road on the right or left. The instructor may also hold the hand pointing up to indicate give way, wave the hand up and down (palm facing towards the floor) to direct the learner to slow down, or move the hand from side-to-side, to direct the learner to park at the side of the road.

INSTRUCTIONS AND DIRECTIONS WHILST STATIONARY

When the learner and the instructor are sitting at the side of the road, communication will be less problematical since many learners will be able to lip read. If this is not possible, then more complicated instructions should be written down. Showing pictures or drawing diagrams can be highly effective. The instructor can use printed cards or flash cards, with the required message displayed (e.g. describing the turn in the road exercise or emergency stop). Simple hand signals can be used to explain or give orders regarding the car's foot controls.

For example, moving a flat right hand to indicate the accelerator, moving a clenched right hand to indicate the brake and moving a flat left hand to indicate the clutch pedal. Raising a flat right hand high into the air will indicate that the learner has applied too much acceleration. Raising a flat left hand high into the air will indicate that the learner has let the clutch come up too far. Raising a clenched right hand high into the air will indicate that the learner has applied too much pressure to the brake.

If a pupil is deaf, increased eye-to-eye contact is essential. Whilst lip reading, deaf people can gain much information from your facial expressions, especially the eyes. Hand gestures and movements are obviously also of greatly increased importance to a deaf pupil. Figures (46 & 47) show hand movements which illustrate whole words commonly used during a driving lesson. Figure (48) illustrates a finger-spelling chart used to convey any other necessary words.

DEMONSTRATING

The instructor should get into the habit of stopping the car more frequently than normal and should demonstrate to the learner as often as possible. Many profoundly deaf learners will experience difficulty moving off from a stationary position (especially on an uphill gradient). This problem arises when there is no Rev. Counter and the learner is unable to set the correct engine speed because he cannot hear the tone of the engine. This problem may be overcome if the learner practices by using his sense of touch in the right foot and hands until he feels the correct vibration through the accelerator and the steering wheel. The instructor should signal to the learner using the "thumbs up" method to indicate that the learner has reached the biting point. Remember, many deaf pupils will learn much quicker if they see a practical demonstration being carried out.

126   DRIVING FOR INSTRUCTORS

DEALING WITH OTHER PROBLEMS
The learner who is hard of hearing
It is particularly important when dealing with a learner who is hard of hearing that the instructor speaks clearly and distinctly. If the surrounding traffic is heavy, even learners with normal hearing may find it difficult to hear and understand instruction. This may cause nervousness and lack of confidence.

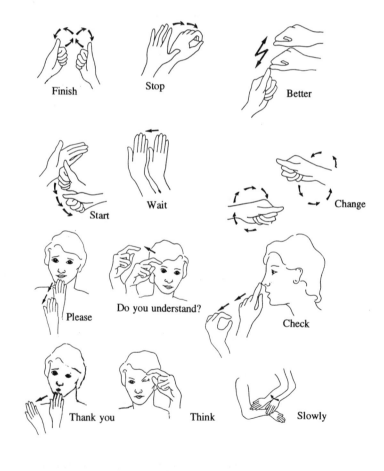

Figure 46. Hand movements to illustrate whole words.

Partial or total loss of sight in one eye

If a driver suffers from loss or partial loss of vision in one eye, moving off from the side of the road can be hazardous. The driver will lack peripheral vision and must therefore look all round and over the shoulder to overcome this problem. Additional mirrors may also be used to give such drivers a much better field of sight. When the car is moving, it is essential that these drivers increase their head movement to see what's happening around them.

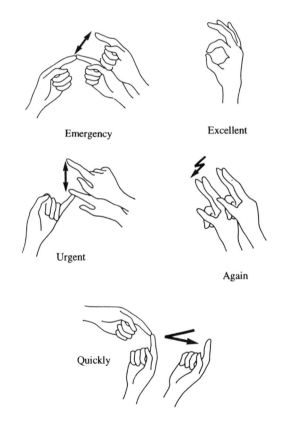

Figure 47. Hand movements to illustrate whole words.

Dyslexia

If a candidate cannot either read or write, suffers from dyslexia (word-blindness), or has any difficulty with the English Language, the learner should receive assistance at home with the Highway Code and other motoring matters from a friend or relative. They should then be tested with verbal questions to judge their level of competence before sitting the theory test. When going to sit the test, let the Driving Standards Agency know if you have any specific disability needs or any form of reading/writing difficulties as special arrangements will be made.

Figure 48. A finger-spelling chart.

APPENDIX

ADI126PT/03
Preset Test Forms

Instructional Test - Part III

The Examiner has marked each aspect of your performance in
columns A and B below. Please see overleaf for explanatory notes.

Candidate's Declaration

I certify that

- the vehicle I have provided for the test is properly insured under the Road Traffic Act 1988 and
- I do/do not have to wear seat belts under the Motor Vehicles (Wearing of Seat Belts) Regulations 1982.

Signed

Date

Centre

Date

Make & model

Reg Mark

Dual Controls   Fitted ☐   Not Fitted ☐

Candidate's Name

Ref. No

Column A

PST No.1 Exercises 1B and 10T

Phase 1-1B Beginner-Controls

	Not Covered	Inadequately Covered	Adequately Covered
Doors	☐	☐	☐
Seat/Head Restraint	☐	☐	☐
Seat Belt	☐	☐	☐
Mirrors	☐	☐	☐
Accelerator	☐	☐	☐
Footbrake	☐	☐	☐
Clutch	☐	☐	☐
Handbrake	☐	☐	☐
Gears	☐	☐	☐
Steering	☐	☐	☐
Indicators	☐	☐	☐
Starting	☐	☐	☐
Precautions before moving off	☐	☐	☐
Normal stop position	☐	☐	☐
Normal stop use of MSM	☐	☐	☐
Normal stop control	☐	☐	☐

Phase 2-10T Trained-Crossroads

	Not Covered	Inadequately Covered	Adequately Covered
Mirror-Signal-Manoeuvre	☐	☐	☐
Speed	☐	☐	☐
Gears	☐	☐	☐
Coasting	☐	☐	☐
Observation	☐	☐	☐
Emerging	☐	☐	☐
Position right	☐	☐	☐
Position left	☐	☐	☐
Pedestrians	☐	☐	☐
Cross approaching traffic	☐	☐	☐
Right corner cut	☐	☐	☐

The results of your test are:

Phase I Grade [   ]   **Phase II Grade** [   ]

Supervising Examiner's name

Location   Section No

S E Signature

Column B

In this column the top line of boxes refer to Phase I and the bottom line of boxes refer to Phase II

1/2/3 = Unsatisfactory   **4/5/6 = Satisfactory**

Fault Assessment

	1	2	3	4	5	6
Identification of faults	☐	☐	☐	☐	☐	☐
Fault analysis	☐	☐	☐	☐	☐	☐
Remedial action	☐	☐	☐	☐	☐	☐

Instructional Techniques

	1	2	3	4	5	6
Level of instruction	☐	☐	☐	☐	☐	☐
Planning	☐	☐	☐	☐	☐	☐
Control of lesson	☐	☐	☐	☐	☐	☐
Communication	☐	☐	☐	☐	☐	☐
Q/A Techniques	☐	☐	☐	☐	☐	☐
Feedback/Encouragement	☐	☐	☐	☐	☐	☐
Instructors use of controls	☐	☐	☐	☐	☐	☐

Instructor Characteristics

	1	2	3	4	5	6
Attitude and Approach to Pupil	☐	☐	☐	☐	☐	☐

ADI 26/PT/01 (Formerly ADI 42/PT/01) Rev 6/95

Instructional Test - Part III

The Examiner has marked each aspect of your performance in columns A and B below. Please see overleaf for explanatory notes.

Candidate's Declaration

I certify that

- the vehicle I have provided for the test is properly insured under the Road Traffic Act 1988 and
- I do/do not have to wear seat belts under the Motor Vehicles (Wearing of Seat Belts) Regulations 1982.

Signed

Date

Centre	
Date	
Make & model	
Reg Mark	
Dual Controls	Fitted ☐ Not Fitted ☐
Candidate's Name	
Ref. No	

Column A

PST No.2 Exercises 2B and 11T

Phase 1-2B Beginner-Moving off / stopping

	Not Covered	Inadequately Covered	Adequately Covered
Briefing on moving off/stopping	☐	☐	☐
Mirrors vision and use	☐	☐	☐
Mirrors, direction, overtaking and stopping	☐	☐	☐
Mirror signal manoeuvre	☐	☐	☐
Precautions before moving off	☐	☐	☐
Co-ordination of controls	☐	☐	☐
Normal stop position	☐	☐	☐
Normal stop control	☐	☐	☐

Phase 2-11T Trained-Meet, cross and overtake other traffic allowing adequate clearance for other road users and anticipation

	Not Covered	Inadequately Covered	Adequately Covered
Mirror-Signal-Manoeuvre	☐	☐	☐
Meet approaching traffic	☐	☐	☐
Cross approaching traffic	☐	☐	☐
Overtake other traffic	☐	☐	☐
Keep a safe distance	☐	☐	☐
Shaving other vehicles	☐	☐	☐
Anticipation of pedestrians	☐	☐	☐
Anticipation of cyclists	☐	☐	☐
Anticipation of drivers	☐	☐	☐

The results of your test are:

Phase I Grade		**Phase II Grade**	

Supervising Examiner's name

Location   Section No

S E Signature

Column B

In this column the top line of boxes refer to Phase I and the bottom line of boxes refer to Phase II

1/2/3 = Unsatisfactory   4/5/6 = Satisfactory

Fault Assessment

	1	2	3	4	5	6
Identification of faults						
Fault analysis						
Remedial action						

Instructional Techniques

	1	2	3	4	5	6
Level of instruction						
Planning						
Control of lesson						
Communication						
Q/A Techniques						
Feedback/Encouragement						
Instructors use of controls						

Instructor Characteristics

	1	2	3	4	5	6
Attitude and Approach to Pupil						

ADI 26/PT/02 (Formerly ADI 42/PT/02) Rev 6/95

Instructional Test - Part III

The Examiner has marked each aspect of your performance in columns A and B below. Please see overleaf for explanatory notes.

Candidate's Declaration

I certify that
- the vehicle I have provided for the test is properly insured under the Road Traffic Act 1988 and
- I do/do not have to wear seat belts under the Motor Vehicles (Wearing of Seat Belts) Regulations 1982.

Signed _____

Date _____

Centre _____

Date _____

Make & model _____

Reg Mark _____

Dual Controls Fitted [ ] Not Fitted [ ]

Candidate's Name _____

Ref. No _____

Column A
PST No.3 Exercises 4P and 7T

Phase 1-4P Partly trained-Turn in the road

	Not Covered	Inadequately Covered	Adequately Covered
Briefing on turn in the road	[ ]	[ ]	[ ]
Co-ordination of controls	[ ]	[ ]	[ ]
Observation	[ ]	[ ]	[ ]
Accuracy	[ ]	[ ]	[ ]

Phase 2-7T Trained-Approaching junctions to turn either right or left

	Not Covered	Inadequately Covered	Adequately Covered
Mirrors	[ ]	[ ]	[ ]
Signal	[ ]	[ ]	[ ]
Brakes	[ ]	[ ]	[ ]
Gears	[ ]	[ ]	[ ]
Coasting	[ ]	[ ]	[ ]
Too fast on approach	[ ]	[ ]	[ ]
Too slow on approach	[ ]	[ ]	[ ]
Position	[ ]	[ ]	[ ]
Pedestrians	[ ]	[ ]	[ ]
Cross approaching traffic	[ ]	[ ]	[ ]
Right corner cut	[ ]	[ ]	[ ]

The results of your test are:

Phase I Grade _____   Phase II Grade _____

Supervising Examiner's name _____

Location _____   Section No _____

S E Signature _____

Column B

In this column the top line of boxes refer to Phase I and the bottom line of boxes refer to Phase II

1/2/3 = Unsatisfactory   4/5/6 = Satisfactory

Fault Assessment

	1	2	3	4	5	6
Identification of faults						
Fault analysis						
Remedial action						

Instructional Techniques

	1	2	3	4	5	6
Level of instruction						
Planning						
Control of lesson						
Communication						
Q/A Techniques						
Feedback/Encouragement						
Instructors use of controls						

Instructor Characteristics

	1	2	3	4	5	6
Attitude and Approach to Pupil						

ADI 26/PT/03 (Formerly ADI 42/PT/03) Rev 6/95

Instructional Test - Part III

The Examiner has marked each aspect of your performance in columns A and B below. Please see overleaf for explanatory notes.

Candidate's Declaration

I certify that
- the vehicle I have provided for the test is properly insured under the Road Traffic Act 1988 and
- I do/do not have to wear seat belts under the Motor Vehicles (Wearing of Seat Belts) Regulations 1982.

Signed

Date

Centre

Date

Make & model

Reg Mark

Dual Controls   Fitted [ ]   Not Fitted [ ]

Candidate's Name

Ref. No

Column A

PST No.4 Exercises 3P and 9T

Phase 1-3P Partly trained-Reversing

Left Reverse [ ]   Right Reverse [ ]

	Not Covered	Inadequately Covered	Adequately Covered
Briefing on reversing	[ ]	[ ]	[ ]
Co-ordination of controls	[ ]	[ ]	[ ]
Observation	[ ]	[ ]	[ ]
Accuracy	[ ]	[ ]	[ ]

Phase 2-9T Trained-T Junctions - Emerging

	Not Covered	Inadequately Covered	Adequately Covered
Mirror-Signal-Manoeuvre	[ ]	[ ]	[ ]
Speed	[ ]	[ ]	[ ]
Gears	[ ]	[ ]	[ ]
Coasting	[ ]	[ ]	[ ]
Observation	[ ]	[ ]	[ ]
Emerging	[ ]	[ ]	[ ]
Position right	[ ]	[ ]	[ ]
Position left	[ ]	[ ]	[ ]
Pedestrians	[ ]	[ ]	[ ]

The results of your test are:

Phase I Grade [ ]   Phase II Grade [ ]

Supervising Examiner's name

Location   Section No

S E Signature

Column B

In this column the top line of boxes refer to Phase I and the bottom line of boxes refer to Phase II

1/2/3 = Unsatisfactory   4/5/6 = Satisfactory

Fault Assessment

	1	2	3	4	5	6
Identification of faults						
Fault analysis						
Remedial action						

Instructional Techniques

	1	2	3	4	5	6
Level of instruction						
Planning						
Control of lesson						
Communication						
Q/A Techniques						
Feedback/Encouragement						
Instructors use of controls						

Instructor Characteristics

	1	2	3	4	5	6
Attitude and Approach to Pupil						

ADI 26/PT/04 (Formerly ADI 42/PT/04)   Rev 6/95

Instructional Test - Part III

The Examiner has marked each aspect of your performance in columns A and B below. Please see overleaf for explanatory notes.

Candidate's Declaration

I certify that

- the vehicle I have provided for the test is properly insured under the Road Traffic Act 1988 and
- I do/do not have to wear seat belts under the Motor Vehicles (Wearing of Seat Belts) Regulations 1982.

Signed

Date

Centre	
Date	
Make & model	
Reg Mark	
Dual Controls	Fitted ☐ Not Fitted ☐
Candidate's Name	
Ref. No	

Column A

PST No.5 Exercises 6P and 8T

Phase 1-6P Partly trained-Emergency stop/Mirrors

	Not Covered	Inadequately Covered	Adequately Covered
Briefing on emergency stop/mirrors	☐	☐	☐
Quick reaction	☐	☐	☐
Use of footbrake/clutch	☐	☐	☐
Skidding	☐	☐	☐
Mirrors vision and use	☐	☐	☐
Mirrors, direction, overtaking and stopping	☐	☐	☐
Mirror-signal-manoeuvre	☐	☐	☐

Phase 2-8T Trained-Progress / Hesitancy - Normal position

	Not Covered	Inadequately Covered	Adequately Covered
Progress too fast	☐	☐	☐
Progress too slow	☐	☐	☐
Hesitancy	☐	☐	☐
Normal position too wide from the left	☐	☐	☐
Normal position too close to the left	☐	☐	☐

The results of your test are:

Phase I Grade		Phase II Grade	
Supervising Examiner's name			
Location		Section No	
S E Signature			

Column B

In this column the top line of boxes refer to Phase I and the bottom line of boxes refer to Phase II

1/2/3 = Unsatisfactory   **4/5/6 = Satisfactory**

Fault Assessment

	1	2	3	4	5	6
Identification of faults						
Fault analysis						
Remedial action						

Instructional Techniques

	1	2	3	4	5	6
Level of instruction						
Planning						
Control of lesson						
Communication						
Q/A Techniques						
Feedback/Encouragement						
Instructors use of controls						

Instructor Characteristics

	1	2	3	4	5	6
Attitude and Approach to Pupil						

ADI 26/PT/05 (Formerly ADI 42/PT/05) Rev 6/95

Instructional Test - Part III

The Examiner has marked each aspect of your performance in columns A and B below. Please see overleaf for explanatory notes.

Candidates Declaration

I certify that
- the vehicle I have provided for the test is properly insured under the Road Traffic Act 1988 and
- I do/do not have to wear seat belts under the Motor Vehicles (Wearing of Seat Belts) Regulations 1982.

Signed

Date

Centre	
Date	
Make & model	
Reg Mark	
Dual Controls	Fitted ☐ Not Fitted ☐
Candidate's Name	
Ref. No	

Column A

PST No.6 Exercises 12P and 5T

Phase 1-12P Partly trained-Pedestrian crossings and the use of signals

	Not Covered	Inadequately Covered	Adequately Covered
Briefing on pedestrian crossings/signals	☐	☐	☐
Mirror-signal-manoeuvre	☐	☐	☐
Speed on approach	☐	☐	☐
Stop when necessary	☐	☐	☐
Overtaking on approach	☐	☐	☐
Inviting pedestrians to cross	☐	☐	☐
Signals by indicator	☐	☐	☐
Signals by arm	☐	☐	☐
Signals - timing	☐	☐	☐
Unnecessary signals	☐	☐	☐

Phase 2-5T Trained-Reverse parking

	Not Covered	Inadequately Covered	Adequately Covered
Briefing on reverse parking	☐	☐	☐
Co-ordination of controls	☐	☐	☐
Observation	☐	☐	☐
Accuracy	☐	☐	☐

The results of your test are:

Phase I Grade [ ]   Phase II Grade [ ]

Supervising Examiner's name

Location [ ]   Section No [ ]

S E Signature

Column B

In this column the top line of boxes refer to Phase I and the bottom line of boxes refer to Phase II

1/2/3 = Unsatisfactory   4/5/6 = Satisfactory

Fault Assessment

	1	2	3	4	5	6
Identification of faults						
Fault analysis						
Remedial action						

Instructional Techniques

	1	2	3	4	5	6
Level of instruction						
Planning						
Control of lesson						
Communication						
Q/A Techniques						
Feedback/Encouragement						
Instructors use of controls						

Instructor Characteristics

	1	2	3	4	5	6
Attitude and Approach to Pupil						

ADI 26/PT/06 (Formerly ADI 42/PT/06) Rev 6/95

Instructional Test - Part III

The Examiner has marked each aspect of your performance in columns A and B below. Please see overleaf for explanatory notes.

Candidates Declaration

I certify that
- the vehicle I have provided for the test is properly insured under the Road Traffic Act 1988 and
- I do/do not have to wear seat belts under the Motor Vehicles (Wearing of Seat Belts) Regulations 1982.

Signed

Date

Centre	
Date	
Make & model	
Reg Mark	
Dual Controls	Fitted ☐ Not Fitted ☐
Candidate's Name	
Ref. No	

Column A

PST No.7 Exercises 7P and 12T

Phase 1-7P Partly trained-Approaching junctions to turn either right or left

	Not Covered	Inadequately Covered	Adequately Covered
Briefing on approaching junctions	☐	☐	☐
Mirrors	☐	☐	☐
Signal	☐	☐	☐
Brakes	☐	☐	☐
Gears	☐	☐	☐
Coasting	☐	☐	☐
Too fast on approach	☐	☐	☐
Too slow on approach	☐	☐	☐
Position	☐	☐	☐
Pedestrians	☐	☐	☐
Cross approaching traffic	☐	☐	☐
Right corner cut	☐	☐	☐

Phase 2-12T Trained-Pedestrian crossings and the use of signals

	Not Covered	Inadequately Covered	Adequately Covered
Mirror-Signal-Manoeuvre	☐	☐	☐
Speed on approach	☐	☐	☐
Stop when necessary	☐	☐	☐
Overtaking on approach	☐	☐	☐
Inviting pedestrians to cross	☐	☐	☐
Signals by indicator	☐	☐	☐
Signals by arm	☐	☐	☐
Signals timing	☐	☐	☐
Unnecessary signals	☐	☐	☐

The results of your test are:

Phase I Grade		Phase II Grade	

Supervising Examiner's name

Location | Section No

S E Signature

Column B

In this column the top line of boxes refer to Phase I and the bottom line of boxes refer to Phase II

1/2/3 = Unsatisfactory   **4/5/6 = Satisfactory**

Fault Assessment

	1	2	3	4	5	6
Identification of faults						
Fault analysis						
Remedial action						

Instructional Techniques

	1	2	3	4	5	6
Level of instruction						
Planning						
Control of lesson						
Communication						
Q/A Techniques						
Feedback/Encouragement						
Instructors use of controls						

Instructor Characteristics

	1	2	3	4	5	6
Attitude and Approach to Pupil						

ADI 26/PT/07 (Formerly ADI 42/PT/07) Rev 6/95

Instructional Test - Part III

The Examiner has marked each aspect of your performance in columns A and B below. Please see overleaf for explanatory notes.

Candidates Declaration

I certify that
- the vehicle I have provided for the test is properly insured under the Road Traffic Act 1988 and
- I do/do not have to wear seat belts under the Motor Vehicles (Wearing of Seat Belts) Regulations 1982.

Signed

Date

Centre

Date

Make & model

Reg Mark

Dual Controls   Fitted [ ]   Not Fitted [ ]

Candidate's Name

Ref. No

Column A

PST No.8 Exercises 9P and 11T

Phase 1-9P Partly trained-T Junctions - Emerging

	Not Covered	Inadequately Covered	Adequately Covered
Briefing on T junctions	[ ]	[ ]	[ ]
Mirror-signal-manoeuvre	[ ]	[ ]	[ ]
Speed	[ ]	[ ]	[ ]
Gears	[ ]	[ ]	[ ]
Coasting	[ ]	[ ]	[ ]
Observation	[ ]	[ ]	[ ]
Emerging	[ ]	[ ]	[ ]
Position right	[ ]	[ ]	[ ]
Position left	[ ]	[ ]	[ ]
Pedestrians	[ ]	[ ]	[ ]

Phase 2-11T Trained-Meet, cross and overtake other traffic allowing adequate clearance for other road users and anticipation

	Not Covered	Inadequately Covered	Adequately Covered
Mirror-Signal-Manoeuvre	[ ]	[ ]	[ ]
Meet approaching traffic	[ ]	[ ]	[ ]
Cross approaching traffic	[ ]	[ ]	[ ]
Overtake other traffic	[ ]	[ ]	[ ]
Keep a safe distance	[ ]	[ ]	[ ]
Shaving other vehicles	[ ]	[ ]	[ ]
Anticipation of pedestrians	[ ]	[ ]	[ ]
Anticipation of cyclists	[ ]	[ ]	[ ]
Anticipation of drivers	[ ]	[ ]	[ ]

The results of your test are:

Phase I Grade [ ]   Phase II Grade [ ]

Supervising Examiner's name

Location   Section No

S E Signature

Column B

In this column the top line of boxes refer to Phase I and the bottom line of boxes refer to Phase II

1/2/3 = Unsatisfactory   4/5/6 = Satisfactory

Fault Assessment

	1	2	3	4	5	6
Identification of faults						
Fault analysis						
Remedial action						

Instructional Techniques

	1	2	3	4	5	6
Level of instruction						
Planning						
Control of lesson						
Communication						
Q/A Techniques						
Feedback/Encouragement						
Instructors use of controls						

Instructor Characteristics

	1	2	3	4	5	6
Attitude and Approach to Pupil						

ADI 26/PT/08 (Formerly ADI 42/PT/08) Rev 6/95

Instructional Test - Part III

The Examiner has marked each aspect of your performance in columns A and B below. Please see overleaf for explanatory notes.

Candidates Declaration

I certify that

- the vehicle I have provided for the test is properly insured under the Road Traffic Act 1988 and
- I do/do not have to wear seat belts under the Motor Vehicles (Wearing of Seat Belts) Regulations 1982.

Signed

Date

Centre

Date

Make & model

Reg Mark

Dual Controls   Fitted☐   Not Fitted☐

Candidate's Name

Ref. No

Column A

PST No.9 Exercises 10P and 12T

Phase 1-10P Partly trained-Crossroads

	Not Covered	Inadequately Covered	Adequately Covered
Briefing on crossroads	☐	☐	☐
Mirror-signal-manoeuvre	☐	☐	☐
Speed	☐	☐	☐
Gears	☐	☐	☐
Coasting	☐	☐	☐
Observation	☐	☐	☐
Emerging	☐	☐	☐
Position right	☐	☐	☐
Position left	☐	☐	☐
Pedestrians	☐	☐	☐
Cross approaching traffic	☐	☐	☐
Right corner cut	☐	☐	☐

Phase 2-12T Trained-Pedestrian crossings and signals

	Not Covered	Inadequately Covered	Adequately Covered
Mirror-Signal-Manoeuvre	☐	☐	☐
Speed on approach	☐	☐	☐
Stop when necessary	☐	☐	☐
Overtaking on approach	☐	☐	☐
Inviting pedestrians to cross	☐	☐	☐
Signals by indicator	☐	☐	☐
Signals by arm	☐	☐	☐
Signals timing	☐	☐	☐
Unnecessary signals	☐	☐	☐

The results of your test are:

Phase I Grade _____   Phase II Grade _____

Supervising Examiner's name

Location _____   Section No _____

S E Signature

Column B

In this column the top line of boxes refer to Phase I and the bottom line of boxes refer to Phase II

1/2/3 = Unsatisfactory   **4/5/6 = Satisfactory**

Fault Assessment

	1	2	3	4	5	6
Identification of faults						
Fault analysis						
Remedial action						

Instructional Techniques

	1	2	3	4	5	6
Level of instruction						
Planning						
Control of lesson						
Communication						
Q/A Techniques						
Feedback/Encouragement						
Instructors use of controls						

Instructor Characteristics

	1	2	3	4	5	6
Attitude and Approach to Pupil						

ADI 26/PT/09 (Formerly ADI 42/PT/09) Rev 6/95

Instructional Test - Part III

The Examiner has marked each aspect of your performance in columns A and B below. Please see overleaf for explanatory notes.

Candidates Declaration

I certify that
- the vehicle I have provided for the test is properly insured under the Road Traffic Act 1988 and
- I do/do not have to wear seat belts under the Motor Vehicles (Wearing of Seat Belts) Regulations 1982.

Signed

Date

Centre

Date

Make & model

Reg Mark

Dual Controls   Fitted [ ]   Not Fitted [ ]

Candidate's Name

Ref. No

Column A

PST No.10 Exercises 11P and 8T

Phase 1-11P Partly trained-Meet, cross and overtake other traffic allowing adequate clearance for other road users and anticipation

	Not Covered	Inadequately Covered	Adequately Covered
Briefing	[ ]	[ ]	[ ]
Mirror-signal-manoeuvre	[ ]	[ ]	[ ]
Meet approaching traffic	[ ]	[ ]	[ ]
Cross other traffic	[ ]	[ ]	[ ]
Overtaking other traffic	[ ]	[ ]	[ ]
Keep a safe distance	[ ]	[ ]	[ ]
Shaving other vehicles	[ ]	[ ]	[ ]
Anticipation of pedestrians	[ ]	[ ]	[ ]
Anticipation of cyclists	[ ]	[ ]	[ ]
Anticipation of drivers	[ ]	[ ]	[ ]

Phase 2-8T Trained-Progress / hesitancy - normal position

	Not Covered	Inadequately Covered	Adequately Covered
Progress too fast	[ ]	[ ]	[ ]
Progress too slow	[ ]	[ ]	[ ]
Hesitancy	[ ]	[ ]	[ ]
Normal position too wide from the left	[ ]	[ ]	[ ]
Normal position too close to the left	[ ]	[ ]	[ ]

The results of your test are:

Phase I Grade [ ]   Phase II Grade [ ]

Supervising Examiner's name

Location   Section No

S E Signature

Column B

In this column the top line of boxes refer to Phase I and the bottom line of boxes refer to Phase II

1/2/3 = Unsatisfactory   4/5/6 = Satisfactory

Fault Assessment

	1	2	3	4	5	6
Identification of faults						
Fault analysis						
Remedial action						

Instructional Techniques

	1	2	3	4	5	6
Level of instruction						
Planning						
Control of lesson						
Communication						
Q/A Techniques						
Feedback/Encouragement						
Instructors use of controls						

Instructor Characteristics

	1	2	3	4	5	6
Attitude and Approach to Pupil						

ADI 26/PT/10 (Formerly ADI 42/PT/10) Rev 6/95

MORE FROM OTTER PUBLICATIONS.......

WHEELS OF JUSTICE (1 899053 02 6, £5.95, 128 pp) by *Duncan Callow*, legal expert with What Car? magazine is packed with essential information. The easy to understand style makes it extremely accessible and contains a useful glossary of terms to clearly spell out all the legal jargon used. *WHEELS OF JUSTICE* is intended as a practical handbook and draws upon many of the author's experiences, both professional and personal. Key areas covered include:

- Insurance
- The MOT and vehicle safety
- Accidents and dealing with their aftermath
- Drink driving and related offences
- The major motoring offences
- The court process
- The fixed penalty system and the penalty points system
- Parking offences and wheel clamping
- Basic motorcycle law
- Driving on the continent
- Buying a used car

"This highly readable law book covers all aspects of driving...useful facts abound". AutoExpress.

"The driver's bible". The News of the World.

BEHIND THE WHEEL: the learner driver's handbook (1 899053 04 2, 264 pp, £7.95), also by *Graham Yuill*, is a step-by-step, highly illustrated handbook. Now into its fourth edition, the book **features a full colour section and questions and answers to help the learner driver learn to drive and pass the theory driving test.** *BEHIND THE WHEEL* will teach the reader all aspects of driving and road safety in 20 easy lessons The teaching methods used are those laid down by The Driving Standards Agency. A completely up-to-date section on trams has also been included. Finally the events of the driving test day are outlined in full with useful advice and tips. **Endorsed by the Driving Instructors Association.**

"Anyone who is learning to drive, or teaching someone else, will appreciate Behind the Wheel". Woman and Home.

BUYING YOUR NEXT CAR: your questions answered (1 899053 07 7, 96 pp, £3.95) is packed with essential information which will help all would-be car buyers of second-hand cars make the right decision. Given that buying a car is the second most expensive purchase that an individual will make, it is vital to get it right. This book contains over one hundred questions. *DON'T BUY A USED CAR UNTIL YOU HAVE READ THIS BOOK - IT MAY WELL SAVE YOU POUNDS!* The key areas covered include:

- How to choose your car
- Finding a genuine used car
- The structural and mechanical assessment
- The test drive
- Used cars and the law
- Coping with dealers and sellers
- Motor vehicle auctions
  Looking after your 'new' car

We are living in an age when violence against car-drivers and theft from cars is on the increase. *ROAD RAGE: the A - Z of motorist's safety* (1 899053 10 7, 96 pp, £4.95) is aimed at every motorist who is concerned about their own personal safety on the road. This essential guide, endorsed by the **DIAmond Advanced Motorists** is packed with vital information and covers:

- Road Rage - Its Causes And Effects.
- The Rights Of A Victim After Attack.
- Recognising Attacks.
- Attack Counter-measures.
- Protecting Your Vehicle.
- Preventing Road Rage And Other Motoring Tips.
- Evasive Manoeuvring Techniques.

Graham Yuill (ADI) is a qualified Department of Transport Driving Instructor and was assigned as personal bodyguard to the Commander of the Royal Irish Regiment for two years. He has passed the Institute of Advanced Motorist's driving test and the Royal Society for the Prevention of Accidents examination.

How to order:-
Through your local bookshop or in case of difficulty, please send a cheque made payable to Otter Publications, of 5 Mosse Gardens, Fishbourne, Chichester, West Sussex, PO19 3PQ.

For Your First

ADI & PDI INSURANCE

HAROLD CONNEW

**IN THE NORTH
FREEFONE
0800 454496**

THE NORTH
OF IRELAND
01247 271333

QUOTE LINES

**IN THE SOUTH
FREEFONE
0800 454337**

BOND LOVIS INSURANCE GROUP

- Free legal policy
- Free loan car (non fault claims)
- Off road tuition
- Previously banned or convicted drivers
- Claims free phone
- Fixed accident excess
- Up to 60% introductory % recommendation scheme
- Pass plus % on private car policies

We guarantee to better any quotation on a like for like basis